RAISE
THE
ROOM

A practical guide to
participant-centered facilitation

Eva Jo Meyers

Table of Contents

When the best leader's work is done,
the people will say, "We did it ourselves."

– Lao Tzu

Raise the Room

A number of years ago, I took on a project to help coordinate mandatory monthly meetings for a group of grantees. As I observed the first meeting, I began to pick up on the cultural norms of the gatherings. For example, most people came in and sat down at tables with other people they already knew. Many people pulled out their laptops and phones and began doing what appeared to be work tasks; activities they continued to do as the meeting started. The hosts of the meeting and their invited guest speakers showed long and elaborate PowerPoint presentations, pausing occasionally to ask if there were any questions and responding quickly to the few people who raised their hands. From my vantage point, it felt like a long update, full of what was actually critical information, but that was landing on half-listening ears.

When I met with the hosts after the meeting, they complained about the disengagement they felt from attendees; not only during the meeting, but in using and implementing the information and resources that were shared. In some cases, they even felt the participants were rebellious. The feeling was that there were two sides, those who were "on board," and those who "just didn't get it."

Over the course of the next year, we began making changes to the meetings. We developed fun and creative ways to encourage people to sit and introduce themselves to people they didn't know. We surveyed people to ask what topics they felt were most pressing, and included time for elective coaching sessions so that people could address those issues within a small community of peers. We integrated hands-on activities to help deliver critical information, so that it was engaging, interactive, and leading toward actionable ways to implement.

We shifted the direction of communication so that the people at the front of the room talked less, and the people in the participant seats talked more.

Needless to say, the change was palpable. People arrived ready to participate and left ready to take action. The dialogue shift went from this:

Participant: "Why is this being done TO me?" Hosts: "Can't you see that this is being done FOR you!"

To this:

Hosts: "What can we do for you today?" Participants: "So glad you asked! We appreciate the time together to share and learn from each other."

If you have picked up this book, chances are you are already in a position of leadership. Transformational Facilitation is born out of Transformational Leadership because of the shared desire to see participants leave our rooms feeling empowered to reach for individual and collectively-created goals, rather than goals we, as leaders, have predetermined for people or that we must push them to reach.

In this framework, being "a teacher" doesn't mean being at the head of a classroom; being "a leader" doesn't mean making all of the decisions; and being "an expert" doesn't mean knowing everything. **What makes a great teacher, leader or expert is their ability to transform the people sitting with them in the room into teachers, leaders, and experts.**

Transformational Facilitation is built on the understanding that our classrooms, organizations, and workplaces are increasingly rich and diverse ecosystems. At the heart of Transformational Facilitation is the value that not only is this diversity important, but that it is indispensable. The ultimate goal of Transformational Facilitation - and this book - is to help you elevate all participants and *"Raise the Room"* through concrete strategies such as enforcing equal airtime, giving decision-making power, and supporting divergent opinions, so that each individual within this diverse ecosystem is fully included, valued, and thriving.

The facilitation model I am presenting here diverges sharply from what I call the "nightly news" model, where one expert tells the rest of us what is going on and what to think. Instead, it shifts us to the "Twitter" model, where each of us is empowered to share the wisdom we bring with us. In this model, we are no longer facilitating "for;" we are facilitating "with." The traditional hierarchy and power dynamics present in our classes, meetings, and events are upended. **There is no teacher, only teaching; there are no leaders, only leading; and there are no experts, only expertise.** When we hear only the voice at the front of the room, we hear only that one voice. When we hand microphones over to everyone in the room, we hear a full symphony.

Doing that well requires practice, courage, and the willingness to honestly reexamine our current ways of operating, because Transformational Facilitation is also based on the belief that if you want to create more innovative, productive, inclusive, and equitable work and learning places, you need to start by modeling. This means making your interactions more innovative, productive, inclusive and equitable at every opportunity. To sum it up: **The WAY we do things is as important as WHAT what we are doing.**

Helping your ecosystems flourish in this way requires thinking more deeply than you probably ever have before about your workshops, meetings,

classes, or events. If you are serious about working towards equity,[1] providing employees or students a voice (and choices), motivating and inspiring the people you work with, or are wanting to make your weekly meetings run more smoothly, then you are probably already aware that the way you facilitate matters.

The challenge now is to take concrete steps to elevate your facilitation skills.

I think it is also important to mention here that shifting your practice toward Transformational Facilitation will not cure your organization or classroom of personal biases, inter-personal conflict, or institutionalized systems of exclusion. Rather, I offer this book, which is evolving up to the moment of printing and will continue to evolve in your hands, as one small area of practice that can be part of a larger organizational or personal goal of increased inclusion.

Towards those ends, this book highlights five areas a facilitator can work toward in order to make transformation happen:
1. Be Prepared
2. Create a Safer Environment
3. Transfer Power to Participants
4. Use Active Learning and Engagement Strategies
5. Motivate Action

This book is divided into five sections according to these areas, with each chapter detailing ways to put the specific area into practice.

Of course, it is an ongoing process! You are not expected to be able to put all of these pieces together at once. At Spark Decks,[2] Oscar Wolters-Duran and I have spent a great deal of time researching and testing the value of micro-practices.

---

[1] In the context of this book, "Equity" means giving people what they need to succeed. In contrast "Equality" is giving everyone the same support regardless of what each individual needs.

[2] Since some of you may not be familiar with Spark Decks, they are a tool designed to help educators and parents learn on-the-job. Each card in a deck contains a little micro-practice - an idea to get you started. Your work as the user is to try out the idea, with your child at home or with your students at school, modifying the activity or practice to suit the children you are working with, and then reflect on how it went afterwards: what worked? what didn't? what did you learn? etc. Oscar Wolters-Duran and I started the company in 2014, and since then we have generated decks on over a dozen different topics, including positive behavior guidance, building social and emotional learning skills, math, literacy, supporting English Language Learners, and more. We are now helping others build decks on topics that matter to their organizations and clients. If you haven't already, definitely check out our website www.spark-decks.com to see what it all looks like.

I love the use of micro-practices because they are each a small, easy-to-manage action you can take toward a goal. For example, as a facilitator, you can decide to simply focus on shaking hands and welcoming everyone into the room at the door before meetings. This tiny practice has the potential to shift the dynamics of your meetings, even without completely overhauling your current practices all at once - which can feel completely overwhelming.

Instead of approaching this book as a curriculum or a system, I encourage you to follow the micro-practices model and pick one or two ideas that really jump out at you to start with. Once you feel comfortable with those and are able to use them automatically, select a few more to try. In addition, the Professional Learning Community Guide at the end of the book is designed to help with pacing if you are using this book with colleagues as part of a community of practice, and the Troubleshooting Guide in the Appendix on page 157, is there to help give you an idea of where to start if you are working through the book on your own.

The planning tools and activities accompanying the text are included to help you generate your own ideas about how these concepts will work in your specific context. I also encourage you to set aside time to reflect after each session you facilitate, using the reflection tool in the Appendix on page 160 to think about how the facilitation went: Did the strategy I tried work? Why or why not? What could I do differently next time? What did I learn?

I applaud you for embarking on this journey. Becoming a Transformational Facilitator is much more difficult than simply running a meeting, workshop, or class. It requires that you, as facilitator, become part of the group you are working with; teaching, learning, leading, following, sharing, and listening along with everyone else. It means giving up control and transferring power; things we struggle to do when faced with deadlines, mandates, and lofty goals. It means setting aside our egos and being open to alternate outcomes. It means believing deeply in the imperative that we must create the conditions for equity to thrive. It is not easy work, but it is transformative.

Good luck to you on this journey and welcome to the community. You are not alone on this path.

NOTES

What We're Talking About

Although there are plenty of people out there who would consider themselves Transformational Facilitators, I want to take a minute to outline exactly what I mean by the term, and other terms used throughout the book.

Facilitator. I use the word "facilitator" to describe anyone who might have an opportunity to get up in front of a group of people to teach, lead, or work with them. The list includes job titles like:

> → manager
> → school principal
> → professor
> → executive director
> → teacher
> → board member
> → coach
> → religious leader
> → project manager
> →
> →
> →
> →

(Use the blank spaces to add in your own job title or others I might have missed!)

Engagement. The activities that can be transformed through facilitation are not just limited to meetings, classes, or workshops, so I call them "engagements" throughout the book. In fact, you may notice that as you begin to practice Transformational Facilitation in one area of your life, it will gradually find its way into other areas.

This has certainly been true for me! As one example, after having facilitated countless workshops and meetings for my work using this method, I joined the board at my son's school. I quickly realized that our parent meetings would benefit from being less "top heavy," and began working with the board to figure out how we could bring Transformational Facilitation into the meetings to improve engagement. I wouldn't be writing this book if it didn't work. My advice? Keep an open mind as you think about where you might apply your Transformational Facilitation skills. You may find the need lurking in very unexpected places.

Here is a partial list of engagements that can benefit from Transformational Facilitation. As you read through the list, think about whether you participate in any of these types of gatherings, and put a check by those that you feel might benefit from a shift. Likewise, you can generate your own list of the events that you attend on a regular basis and think about which ones might benefit from this method. I've left a few empty spaces so you can add in your own ideas!

Work-Related:

- ❏ One-on-one check-ins
- ❏ New hire orientations
- ❏ College courses
- ❏ Annual staff evaluations
- ❏ Weekly/monthly staff meetings
- ❏ Team retreats
- ❏ Event planning
- ❏ Strategic planning meetings
- ❏ Volunteer orientations or trainings
- ❏ After school classes
- ❏ Board meetings
- ❏
- ❏

Personal:

- ❑ Parent-teacher conferences
- ❑ Family gatherings
- ❑ Clubs or hobby group classes or associations
- ❑ PTA meetings
- ❑ Religious group meetings
- ❑ Children's club meetings (e.g. 4-H, Girl Scouts, Little League, etc.)
- ❑ Support group meetings
- ❑
- ❑
- ❑

Transformational Facilitation. Transformational Facilitation is based on the tenets of Transformational Leadership, in which a leader inspires and engages employees (or whomever that leader happens to be leading) toward a common goal and shared vision. In essence, this practice flips the traditional notion that a leader is at the top, with everyone else following along, and puts those "followers" into the driver's seat.

To understand what this means, let's compare events that use Transformational Facilitation with events that are run in traditional ways; The following chart highlights a few key differences:

Traditional Facilitation	Transformational Facilitation
The facilitator is there to share information with the group.	The facilitator is there to help participants discover and share their own wisdom.
The facilitator generates and drives the outcomes, in which there is a clear hierarchy.	The group shapes the outcomes, everyone is a contributor, and the group has intentional balance and equity.
The facilitator's voice is heard most during the event.	The facilitator's voice is rarely heard during the event.
Outcomes of the event are one-directional sharing of information (mostly from facilitator to participants).	Outcomes of the event include shared learning and communal problem-solving around the topics.
Done TO participants.	Done WITH participants.
The mood is serious and quiet, and not everyone is fully engaged.	The mood is active and everyone is fully engaged.
People are sitting in rows, or maybe around a boardroom table.	People are circled up and moving around often.
The facilitator wields a dry erase marker or PowerPoint slide advancer.	Everyone is writing and creating visuals.

Of course, life is never completely black-and-white. You may have a traditional engagement that has elements of Transformational Facilitation within it, and vice-versa. In fact, I would say that even my own events still contain elements of traditionally facilitated engagements, because even I have not fully mastered the ability to be completely transformative. Yet.

One key idea to remember when you are leading an event with Transformational Facilitation that makes it completely different from plain-old facilitation is that you are a role model. The strategies you are using are not just for the benefit of your participants in the moment, but will hopefully, if done well and with transparency, be replicated by participants in their own engagements that they lead. That's what makes it truly Transformational, and not just some cool, hip strategy.

Now, before moving on, consider taking a minute to use the graphic organizer to brainstorm what Transformational Facilitation means to you and how you might use it to **transform** your current situation.

S - Success: What would make me feel successful?

 P - Problems: What are my current challenges?

 A - Alternatives and Actions: What options are available and interesting to me to address my challenges? What can I do/change?

 R - Resources: What strengths, allies, or tools do I already have?

 K - Keep: Which of the possible actions or alternatives will I try?

NOTES

Overcoming Your FOF (Fear of Facilitation)

Before I begin addressing strategies to help you as a Transformational Facilitator, I feel it is important to take a moment to address you, as a person. So, hello there!

FOF is a real thing. In fact, many of the most competent facilitators I know have admitted to me that they get terribly nervous prior to stepping in front of a group of people. I was floored at these revelations because I would never have guessed. These facilitators always seem so calm, cool, and collected. So organized. So masterful.

My suspicion is also that a few of you reading this may never have expected to find yourself in a position where you are required to facilitate. You love math and became a math professor. You were a great teacher and became a principal. You were an excellent employee and became a boss. And, let's face it, certain audiences can even shake me up. So, if this resonates with you, here is a collection of ideas to help you address your fear, push through it (over and over again!), and move on to the important work you are facilitating.

❏ **Dissolve the hierarchy**. What makes me most nervous is facilitating a room full of people who I consider to be "more important" or "more powerful" than I am. This idea is usually related to their job titles, but it can sometimes also be attached to how well they know each other, how familiar they are with the material, or what past criticisms I remember. My strategies for getting past this FOF are to:

→ Remind myself that I wouldn't be in a position of facilitating this group if someone, somewhere didn't trust me to do it well;

→ Introduce myself to every person in the room individually before the event starts so that I can get to know them as humans, not just as their title or who I have built them up to be; and

→ Be transformative! Meaning, I start off the event by introducing myself and calling attention to my role as facilitator, not as a master of content, experience, or their learning, and stay focused on that. If there's a question I cannot answer, it goes onto the "Parking Lot" for later, or gets put back on the group to answer for itself. I don't need to know everything! We're all just people learning together.

❏ **Admit your discomfort**. I'm not a huge fan of over-sharing, but let's remember that there's a very high chance that most of the people in front of you are feeling a little uneasy themselves. Think about the last class, meeting, or workshop you attended. Did you feel comfortable from the moment you walked in the room? Let your participants know that you'll be starting the engagement by "warming up the room," then run an icebreaker that you participate in as well. If you want, you can even ask people to check in with themselves before you start: On a scale from 1-10, how comfortable are they feeling right now? After you run the icebreaker, ask them to rate their comfort levels again. Did they go up? Did yours go up? Own it!

❑ **Be prepared and practiced**. Make yourself a checklist of everything you will need to run your engagement, then pack your bags and boxes up the night before. Run through your agenda a couple of times like you would a script for a play. Take every opportunity to get up in front of a group and facilitate, because you can't get better if you don't put yourself out there.

❑ **Own your script.** Plan out each minute in detail on your Facilitator's Agenda, (covered in Chapter 4), then read through it a few times to internalize the flow in the days and hours beforehand. Try new strategies, but sandwich them between strategies you already feel comfortable using.

❑ **Be yourself.** I cannot stress this one enough. Don't dress a certain way (for me, that would be in heels and makeup - two things that make me extremely uncomfortable) just because you think it will make an impression. You don't need to prove that you are something more than or different from who you are. Like to tell dumb jokes? Tell 'em! (I always do.) Did your favorite song just come on in your pre-workshop playlist? Dance to it! Love to sip on a smoothie in the morning? Bring it! Besides the fact that Transformational Facilitation is based on authenticity, giving yourself permission to JUST. BE. YOU. will take away a lot of the jitters that can occur when you are trying to live up to someone else's expectations or projections of who you "should" be.

❑ **Ask for feedback**. The truth can sometimes be painful, especially when you know something

didn't go as well as you hoped it would, but letting people know that they will have an opportunity to provide feedback on your facilitation at the end of the session is also a chance to let people know that you are continually striving to learn and grow - just as you hope they will do in the course of your time with them. Plus, people sometimes write really nice things. I save my favorites and read them to myself when I need a little "pep talk" before an engagement. My favorite to this day: "Eva can make watching paint dry a palatable experience." Yessssssss! (More on this topic can be found in Chapter 52.)

❑ **Plan the post-party**. Facilitating can be stressful, especially for a new group or a long day or series of days. Plan something fun for after the engagement so that you have something to look forward to. If being around people all day is exhausting to you, plan a quiet evening at home. If you experience a few tense or nerve-wracking moments while facilitating, take a deep breath and remind yourself, "There's ice cream at the end of this!"

Now remember, you don't need to do all of these. Just check off the one or two you want to try first and come back to the rest later. Take a minute to use the graphic organizer on the following page to reflect on what your fears are about being a facilitator and what you might do to work through those fears. Being afraid is simply part of caring about yourself and the people around you. Send yourself some love, roll up your sleeves, and jump on in!

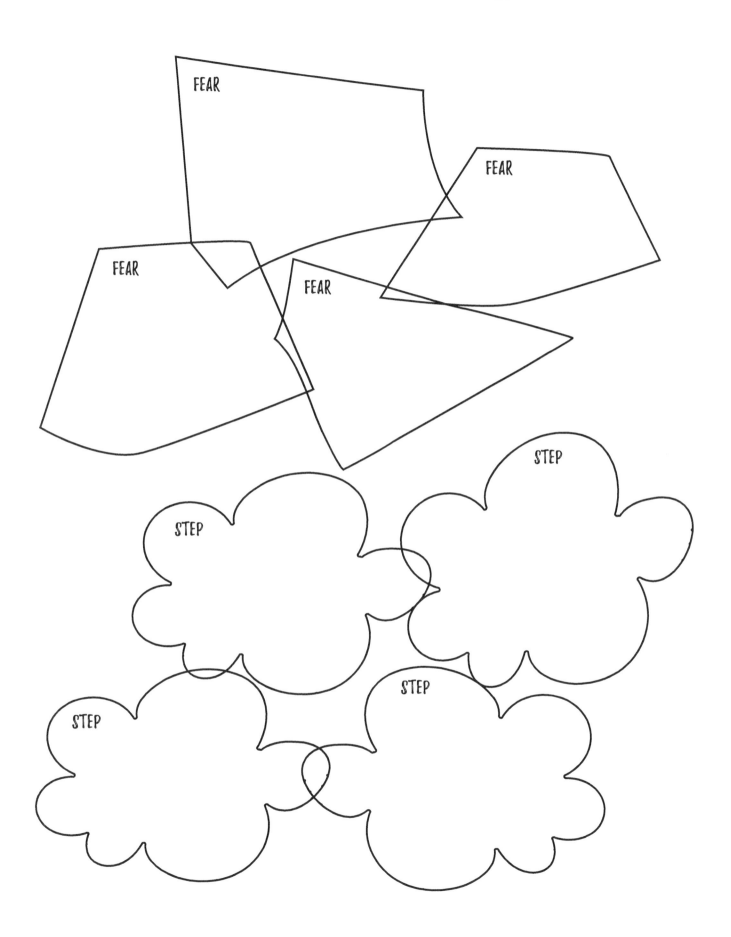

NOTES

SECTION ONE
BE PREPARED

In its essence, being prepared is about getting yourself AND your participants ready. When this is done well, your event will feel like it is running itself. While you cannot prepare for every possibility, you can mitigate a lot of stress by thinking through exactly how you are going to show up and facilitate. Think of it as looking at a map and checking out a guidebook before you embark on a vacation in another city. The more you know, and therefore the better you plan, the more smoothly your engagement will run.

It is tempting to underplan.

- ❏ If you usually spend ten minutes creating a meeting agenda, spend an hour on your next agenda.

- ❏ After the meeting, reflect:
- → Did the extra planning make a difference?

- → If so, what kind of difference did you notice?

- → If not, why do you think it didn't make a difference to be better prepared?

I used to show up to meetings and workshops about 70% prepared. I'd usually have decent goals and objectives on paper and a general idea of what I would cover under each bullet point I'd outlined. I was good enough. As soon as I started co-facilitating workshops and meetings with my colleague, Oscar,

that all went out the window; you can't run a two-person show without a script. And once you start working off a script for your meetings or workshops, you will never go back, because the quality of your engagements will increase exponentially (more on this in Chapter 4). Being prepared in this way assures that your points will come across clearly to participants, and, perhaps even more importantly, shows them that you care enough about what is happening in the room to have done such a thorough job getting ready for them. They know you are prepared and engaged, and they rise to meet your level of commitment.

Transformational Facilitators can sometimes almost seem invisible during a meeting or workshop, but they still always hold the space because they have spent the hours prior to the engagement constructing it.

Being prepared also means getting yourself into the right mental and physical state to show up 100% for your participants. I've organized dozens of conferences over the years, and, at the events, people always comment to me with surprise, "You seem so calm!" because I'm not running around and in a sweat. And I feel good and am having fun, most importantly. That's what being prepared does.

By now I hope you're wondering how, exactly, to prepare so that you, too, can be the calm, cool, collected facilitator who has everyone's rapt attention. Alright then, let's get started.

NOTES

CHAPTER 1
Get to Know Your Audience

If you don't already work with the people you will be facilitating, the first thing to do is to get to know your audience. (If you already know everyone, because you are their supervisor, for example, you might still want to read this chapter, because you can always learn more about people!)

There are three basic things you really want to know:

1. Who is going to be in the room?
2. What are their needs?
3. What are they expecting to get out of their time with you?

Even now, all too often, I leave a workshop feeling like I didn't get to know the participants well enough. Truly hearing and seeing your participants is imperative for being able to move them toward action and deep learning. First and foremost, you are dealing with real human beings.

How can you best get to know your audience? This depends on your particular situation. Here are some thoughts and potential action items for you as you are thinking about how you will get to know the people you will be facilitating.

❑ **Use surveys.** If I am going to be running a conference or professional development opportunity for a large group, I like to use a survey. The trick with surveys is to either make them part of the registration process, so that everyone is obligated to complete them, and/or to keep them very short.

Some open-ended, qualitative questions you might consider asking include:

→ What motivated you to sign up for this event?

→ What do you hope to be able to do as a result of attending this event?

→ What type of environment, activities, or support will help you feel most comfortable at the event?

→ What resources related to [topic] are you already using?

Quantitative questions you might add include:

→ On a scale from 1-10, how familiar are you already with [topic]?

→ Please check which topics you are most interested in having us cover during the event [list possible topics]

→ Are you interested in leading, or co-leading, a session during the event?

If you are doing this as part of a registration process, you can ask demographic questions to help you understand who will be participating. These include job titles, employers, number of years in the field, etc. If I am doing a workshop on Staff Supervision, I'd like to know how many years the participant has been supervising, how many people they supervise, and whether they see their role primarily as a coach, manager, or mentor.

You might also try to incorporate survey questions that you can work into your event in some way. For example, for a recent learning event I hosted for a client, I asked participants in the registration survey what their "superpower" on the topic was. I turned their responses into a slideshow that ran while they had lunch. It was fun to see them reading the slides and, subconsciously or consciously, knowing that their voices were being highlighted.

One thing to keep in mind when administering a pre-event survey is that the survey sets participant expectations. If you ask whether someone is a vegetarian or not and they click "yes," they will expect a vegetarian meal option. Similarly, if you ask for input on what topics to cover during the event, it is helpful to be transparent when you set your agenda, and let everyone know that the topics were selected based on participant input.

❑ **Hold focus groups or interviews.** These are a great way to get to know your audience prior to creating your agenda. As with the surveys, think about what questions will help you best plan for your event, keeping in mind that the questions you ask and the conversations you have prior to the event in large part become part of the event itself; you are setting the bed in which you will later plant the seeds.

With focus groups or interviews, you do not need to speak with everyone who will be attending. These can be done with a subset of participants; ideally, a representative subset. For example, if you will be doing a school-wide professional learning event, try to speak with at least one teacher, one administrator, and one support staff member. Ask the same or similar questions to gauge how you may need to tailor the event for each group of participants.

As with the surveys, be transparent with participants about the focus groups and interviews. In fact, you may even want to spend time at the start of the event to share back what was shared with you, and point out how you will be using the information to guide the content and process of the engagement. You may even feel drawn to thank the focus group members or interviewees for their feedback and and/or show your gratitude to them in some public way.

❑ **Make individual contacts.** Especially for smaller workshops, I find that my only point of contact is the person coordinating the event on behalf of

the client. This is less than ideal, but if there is no way to be in touch directly with participants prior to the event, I try to ask my point of contact as many questions as I can, such as:

→ Is this event mandatory?

→ Why are you bringing in this topic/me as a facilitator?

→ What other engagements has your staff participated in recently?

→ How does this engagement fit in with the mission of your agency?

❑ **Do observations or site visits.** Another great way to get to know your participants is by observing them at work. This is particularly easy if you are going to be running an engagement for people that you already supervise, since you most likely work in the same place. But even if you don't already work with the audience, you can ask to see what their situation is like on a site visit. What is the work or learning environment like? Can you see why you are being brought in to run a meeting or do a workshop on the proposed topic? Let yourself be seen, and, if at all possible, introduce yourself and explain why you are observing their work environment. Casual conversations during an on-site visit can offer a great deal of insight into your audience.

❑ **Learn it in real time.** If you have no way of getting to know who will be participating in your event prior to the event itself, you can still get to know people by being available as they arrive. I always walk around a workshop or meeting room and extend a handshake, ask where a person is attending from, why they are there, and what they are hoping to leave with. Even being able to do this with a handful of participants can be very informative, and it sets a great tone by showing that you are curious about the people in the room. Plus, if you're like me, you're probably genuinely curious.

Asking questions is an underlying theme of the Transformational Facilitation model. Getting to know your audience is all about asking good, meaningful questions. The answers that you find yourself with are vital for crafting your agenda. Practice asking these getting-to-know you questions, and then practice using the responses intentionally by referring back to the responses during your engagement. (For example, if a participant has told me they are attending because they are interested in learning to cook, when we get to the part of the agenda that talks about cooking, I might say something like, "Shana is here because she is interested in learning to cook, so now we are going to get to that part of our agenda!")

After each event, reflect on what information would have been helpful to know prior to the event. Make a note so that you remember to ask those questions next time. As with everything else in this book, getting to know your audience is an iterative process. Try something out, notice what works and what doesn't, adjust, and do it again.

NOTES

CHAPTER 2
Set Clear Goals and Objectives

An agenda has a lot of moving parts, which is why developing crystal clear goals and objectives is so important. When done well, these become the guidepost around which everything else revolves. Meetings, workshops, or events without clear goals and objectives have a tendency to pick up momentum, veer off topic, and take a lot longer than they need to. Returning to your well-crafted and intentional goals and objectives helps you stay on course and avoid these pitfalls. This chapter covers some ideas about how to create sturdy goals and objectives so that you can build your agenda solidly on them.

❑ **Know the difference.** When I started running meetings, I distinctly remember being unclear about the difference between a goal and an objective. What I've come to understand is that a goal is an overarching theme.

Example of **goals** are:

→ The goal of this meeting is to collectively make several key decisions about fundraising for the coming year.
→ The goal of this workshop is to help participants share and learn strategies for handling confrontational situations with students.
→ The goal of this event is to bring stakeholders together to identify solutions to common problems.

The **objectives**, then, break down what that will look like, and actually follow your agenda. They start with, *"By the end of this meeting/ workshop, participants will…"*

Using the first example above, about fundraising, the objectives might read:

→ Decide whether to hold one or two major donor events this summer;
→ Calendar solicitation mail-out dates;
→ Brainstorm and select newsletter topics for the remainder of the year.

In our second example, about student confrontations they might include:
→ Identify when and where most confrontations take place;
→ Brainstorm and strategizes ways to mitigate confrontations;
→ Decide on three key strategies they will try this month, and be prepared to report back at our next meeting.

❑ **Remember that less is more.** Limit yourself to one overarching goal and no more than 3-5 objectives, even for a full-day meeting; trying to do too much can overwhelm and disempower participants. You may already be familiar with "SMART" goals. The section at the end of this chapter offers a refresher in case you have forgotten. Now is a good time to get acquainted with what they are and how you can employ them. I have found "SMART" goals to be extremely useful in enabling participants to follow – and lead – a clear path along with you.

❑ **Evaluate your progress.** We will discuss how to evaluate your meetings and workshops in Chapter 52, but I want to mention here that the goals and objectives you create can be directly inserted into your evaluation wording, enabling you to check on how well your group felt that the goals and objectives were met. For example, if one of my stated objectives was to "give participants an opportunity to learn from, and share with, their colleagues," in my evaluation I will include a question that asks, "Did you learn from and/or share with your colleagues?" I often find myself surprised when participants rate one of the objectives as "not being met" on an evaluation when I felt it was. Often, this is because my objective was more clear in my mind than it was on paper or the activity we did to meet that objective didn't quite land.

❑ **Include both "experiential" and "rational" or "practical" aims**. This distinction is something I learned when I went to a workshop to become a Technology of Participant (ToP) facilitator.[3] It is a useful distinction for a Transformational Facilitator because we are working not just on the "let's get this done" plane, but also on the "let's get this done in a way that engages people from the heart" level. Here are some examples:

❑ **Experiential** goals/objectives are about how participants feel or experience the event. They might include:

> → Participants will build trust with their team
> → Participants will feel motivated to get started on the project
> → Participants will have fun

❑ **Rational/Practical** goals/objectives are centered on what people will learn or be able to do. They might include:

> → Participants will be able to use SMART goals when creating agendas
> → Participants will share and evaluate strategies for crowd-sourced fundraising
> → Participants will understand what a Transformational Facilitator is

Crafting well-worded, succinct, and SMART goals and objectives is a great skill to work on and is well worth your time. Edit and revise your goals and objectives until you are sure they accurately state what you intend to cover. If you are co-planning your meeting or class, send the goals and objectives to your counterpart to make sure you are on the same page before you delve into how you will cover the material. Once your goals and objectives are set in stone, you can begin to build your agenda accordingly.

I encourage you to create goals and objectives (and agendas) even for short phone meetings or one-on-ones and notice what happens.

Do participants seem more relaxed?

_____

_____

Do they (and you) have a greater sense of accomplishment after the engagement?

_____

_____

Do you feel like you are getting more done?

_____

_____

Try it and see!

---

[3] The Technology of Participation (ToP) provides structured facilitation methods to help groups think, talk, and work together. Learn more at https://www.top-network.org.

SMART Goals (and Objectives)

The acronym "SMART" first appeared on the scene in the 1980s in an article by George Doran in the magazine, *Management Review*.[4] Since it was first introduced, there have been many iterations of what each letter stands for. The interpretation I outline below is the most popular.

S = Specific. It is very easy to create loose goals for your engagement. Setting a specific goal or objective means you have to sit down and think about what you are really looking to accomplish with the event. A good rule of thumb when creating *specific* goals or objectives is to ask yourself a bunch of "wh" questions – When? Where? Why? Who?

Do a brainstorm to get all of your ideas down about what you hope to accomplish in the event using the "wh" questions, and then narrow it down to one sentence.

Returning to our examples above, our fundraising meeting goal is "to collectively make several key decisions about fundraising for the coming year." A less thought-out goal might have been, "Discuss fundraising activities." I'm exaggerating a little here, but you can see how this misses the mark because you are not going to "discuss," you are doing to "decide." You are also going to decide "collectively," which is why this meeting needs to be called; it's hard to make collective decisions without getting together. You're also not just making decisions about fundraising activities, but will be focusing on "key" activities, making this more specific than if you were going to be open to *all* fundraising activities.

These may seem like insignificant differences, but they set the tone and direction more clearly than a general goal would. This becomes extremely important later, as you create an agenda that you plan to keep on course.

M = Measurable. Measurable goals and objectives are easily quantifiable. This often looks like putting in numbers, so we have:

"Decide whether to hold one or two donor events this summer,"

rather than just,

"Decide on our donor event(s) for the summer."

The latter objective could lead to all kinds of tangents, like the theme, location, etc., that could eat up a lot of time in the meeting, when what you really need to focus on is whether to have one or two events.

Or, "Identify when and where most confrontations take place,"

rather than simply,

"Talk about confrontations."

In this example, your objective leads you to the creation of a critical set of data, rather than just a general discussion about confrontations that may not lead anywhere productive.

Measurable objectives help keep participants motivated, because they can see the progress of their efforts ("We decided to only have one donor event this summer!"), which is an extremely important part of Transformational Facilitation.

Good questions to ask yourself as you are aiming to make your goals measurable are:

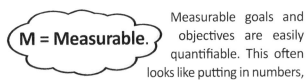

→ How much?
→ How long?
→ How many?

---

4 (Doran)

I often create my objectives, and then go back through them to make sure they are measurable, adding wording to make them quantifiable as I edit as in the examples above.

A = Achievable. This is a big one. Will we be able to eliminate confrontations altogether? No. That would not be an achievable goal. However, we *can* "share and learn strategies" toward reducing confrontations. Will we be able to create a whole fundraising plan in one meeting? Maybe, but probably not unless it's a full day retreat. Keeping your goals and objectives achievable helps participants walk away with a sense of accomplishment from the event. We came to do X, and we did it!

I am notorious for trying to squeeze too much into meetings and workshops. I am still learning how to be honest with myself about how much can be accomplished in the time allotted. A lot of this depends on who your participants are and how skillfully you are able to move them toward decisions and actions.

When thinking about making your goals and objectives achievable, take a few minutes to consider:

→ Who is in the room and what can they do?
→ Will you have to spend time sharing background information and getting people caught up, or does this group already have the tools they will need?
→ Will this particular group of participants have the knowledge, power, and/or skill to accomplish the goal or make decisions?

Which brings us to the next letter.

R = Relevant. This goes back to the part about getting to know your audience. There is nothing worse than walking into a workshop and realizing that it has nothing to do with your job or your needs, or that the issues you are being asked to tackle are outside of your control.

Making your goals and objectives relevant is key in Transformational Facilitation because participants need to feel like what is taking place in your event matters and is useful. **I cannot underscore enough the importance of having participants walk out of your meeting or workshop feeling like they have concrete action items and tools, or have gained clarity around a topic, decision, or timeline.** Doing a workshop on reducing student confrontations with a group of participants who don't regularly experience this problem is a waste of everyone's time.

I'd also like to insert a cautionary note here about meetings, specifically. Sometimes we add agenda items or objectives to a meeting that are actually announcements, rather than things that need the time and space of a meeting to address. This can feel boring and like a waste of time for participants, even if the topic is relevant to their jobs. When thinking about making your goals and objectives *relevant*, consider not just the topic, but also whether this is an item that requires face-to-face time. You may find that in actuality, the item can be covered in a written "Updates" section of your agenda instead, as we will discuss more fully when we get to agendas in Chapter 4.

T = Time Bound. Put simply, this means that your goals and objectives should be clear about *when*. Is this something happening today, or in the next month or year? Our first goal example is explicit about this, "The goal of this meeting is to collectively make several key decisions about fundraising for *the coming year*." Likewise, "Decide on three key strategies they will try this month," and "Be prepared to report back at our next meeting," are both examples of time-bound objectives.

Each time you begin preparing for an engagement, run through your goals and objectives to see if they are SMART by pausing at each letter and asking yourself if it meets the criteria:

❑ Specific
❑ Measureable
❑ Achievable
❑ Relevant
❑ Time Bound

CHAPTER 3
Prepare Participants

As you probably suspect by now, facilitating a successful meeting or workshop starts before the engagement itself. You can probably remember a time when you arrived as a participant to a conference or meeting already thinking about the event on your way *to* the event, or even for a few days or weeks beforehand. You probably already had some emotional attachments, too: nervousness, eagerness, resistance, hope. In fact, if you really think about it, this is probably true about every meeting or event you attend.

As a Transformational Facilitator, you can help to ensure success *during* the engagement by reaching out to participants prior to the actual event. The more information you can provide, the more you can set a tone of welcoming and excitement, the more comfortable and eager your participants will be. And having a room full of people in front of you who are in the right mindframe goes a long way toward ensuring a successful engagement.

Here are a few ideas on how to prepare participants:

- ❏ **Be clear on logistics**. Send out an email with location information at least a week prior to the event. Include details about parking, public transportation, accessibility, etc. I usually include links to parking garages, bus routes, and maps. If you are covering the cost of parking, or travel, definitely mention that and the process for reimbursement!

- ❏ **Outline the hospitality**. In the same email (or a separate email) include information about what to expect in terms of hospitality. For example:

> → We will be starting promptly at 10am, so please plan to arrive a few minutes early to sign in, grab some of the hot coffee and pastries we will be providing, and find a seat.
> → I also like to include information about dress, e.g. "Dress code is casual for this engagement, but the temperature in Oakland can fluctuate greatly during the day, so bringing layers is recommended."
> → Of course, include lots of information about the food you will (or will not) be providing, "You will have an hour lunch break. Attached please find a list of local restaurants and cafes where you can go to enjoy a meal with your colleagues."

- ❏ **Share the agenda**. If you don't want to share all of the minute details of your agenda, at least make sure you share key times (e.g. registration time, starting time, lunch time, conclusion time) along with the goals and objectives. Understanding when things are happening may seem like a small detail, but people really appreciate knowing when breaks will be and that the day is clearly mapped out. Same goes for the goals and objectives: it is really comforting to people to know what will be covered; it helps activate their curiosity, and puts them in the mindset of the topic.

- ❏ **Create a connection**. In all of your communication, make sure you are sending the message that you are excited and looking forward to learning and sharing with the attendees. Read and reread your emails, putting yourself in the place of a participant. Do you sound warm and welcoming or do you sound all business? Let participants know that they can contact you with questions, and provide your cell number or another easy way for them to get in touch if they are running late or are lost on the day of the event. These small gestures make you accessible and create a feeling of importance for the participants.

If your participants are people you see on a regular basis (e.g. people you supervise), you can also remind them of your excitement in person, as in, "I'm really looking forward to our team brainstorming session tomorrow!" You don't want to be disingenuous, but enthusiasm is contagious. If you roll your eyes every time the engagement is mentioned, or act stressed out about it, that will spread to your participants. Which brings me to my final point about preparing participants...

❑ **Prepare *yourself*.** Make sure YOU know where you are going, where to park, what materials will be available to you at the venue, etc. There is nothing worse than arriving to an event having not yet had your coffee, only to realize that not only is no coffee being served, but there isn't a nearby cafe around!

I realize this may seem like a lot of extra work, but I guarantee that in the long run, it will make your engagement run much more smoothly and will save you a lot of time and effort on the actual day.

NOTES

CHAPTER 4
Craft an Agenda

A Transformational Facilitator needs to bring together many important elements to be effective. Being able to craft a clear, meaningful agenda is what pulls all of those important pieces together. This is the document from which everything flows. When the agenda is done well, the event will run itself. When rushed or left partially completed, it is like trying to use a treasure map where crucial parts have been erased. I usually set aside at least one hour of planning time to work on my agenda for each hour of the actual meeting. The truth is, the time it takes me to craft my agenda is often longer than the time I spend actually running the engagement itself (meaning, it might take me two hours to create the agenda for a one-hour meeting!).

Here are some ideas about things to think about as you build your agenda:

❑ **Give yourself time and space to think creatively.** Here I am, sitting in front of my computer, with all my notes about who will be in the room and what they want to cover. Now I need to come up with a way to make that happen. It is easy to see that writer's block can quickly set in. Make sure you are not rushed or constantly being interrupted as you set out to create your agenda. Mark off time in your calendar, put up a "do not disturb" sign, escape to a café - do everything you can to give yourself room to think creatively and thoroughly. It is that important.

❑ **Generate a useful format.** By "format" I mean the actual way that your agenda appears on paper. I used to just write down my goals, objectives, and then some bullet points about what I would be covering. If I felt extra fancy, I would add in approximate times. I might jot down a few notes about what I wanted to make sure to cover under each bullet point, and I would even add some thoughts on how I planned to deliver the content.

I have learned that putting *everything* down on paper not only makes my events more thoroughly thought-out and therefore smoother, but also helps me stay on track; even when the going gets rough I have my highly detailed road map in front of me to guide me. Plus, it's easy to read and find things, which is important when you have 50 people in front of you waiting to hear the instructions for the next activity.

I start my documents with the title of the event, the date, location, and the start/end times. If you run a lot of meetings or workshops, you will immediately understand why this is so important; there is nothing worse than showing up to an engagement with the wrong Facilitator's Agenda in hand! Since I also like to file hard copies of my agendas, this makes it easy to find them again, for those times when I reuse them.

Next, I insert the goals and objectives of the event. It is helpful to have these right at the top.

My favorite agenda format these days is a table as in the example below. The first column contains the time, written out as start and end times AND length (e.g. 9am - 9:15am, 15 minutes). In the second column I put the title and purpose of that section, along with the steps in full detail. In the last column, I include what materials or handouts I will need to carry out the section:

Time	Activity	Materials

9:00 - 9:15am *(15 min)*	**Welcome and Introductions**
	
	Purpose: Participants will be welcomed into the meeting and learn who is in the room.
	
	Steps:
	1. Introduce myself and the title of today's workshop
	2. Direct everyone to the handouts, make sure everyone has all of the materials
	3. Invite each participant to briefly introduce themselves by sharing:
	  a. What is your name?
	  b. Where do you work?
	  c. What is your role there?
		❑ Participant handout packets

❑ **Make it legible**. Think about the font type and size (a small curvy script might look nice, but can be difficult to follow). Use consistent bullets. Highlight or bold parts that you really want to make sure you point out or cover. Number your pages (oh, that time when I had a super long agenda that I stapled together completely out of order - not fun!). I follow a rule of thumb that anyone should be able to pick up my agenda and follow it. Use that as a litmus test with your next agenda and see how legible you can make it!

❑ **Refer to it**. Do not be afraid to look at your agenda. This is not a play; you do not need to memorize it! There is no use in taking all of that time to create a masterpiece only to forget a critical piece because you were too embarrassed or nervous to take a minute to refer to your guiding document!

❑ **Post and share it**. I have recently started to use a new format for posting my agendas that I learned at a conference. Rather than simply writing the agenda items up on a whiteboard, PPT, or handing out a sheet, I now use large sticky notes to create three columns, and additional sticky notes for each agenda item. It looks like this.

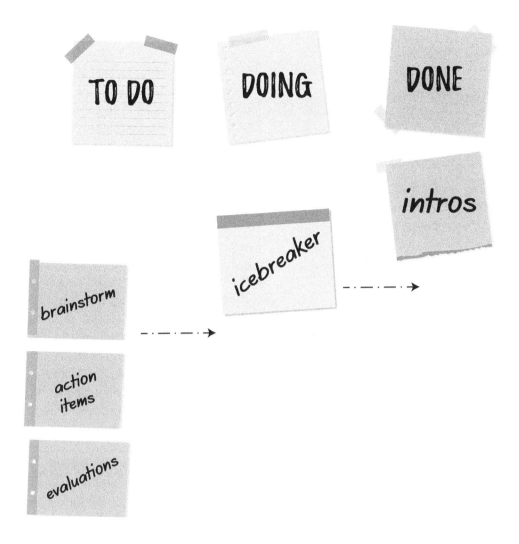

As I move through the agenda, I move each item into the "Doing" and then "Done" category, until, by the end of the event, all of the items have been moved into the "Done" column on the far right. Talk about feeling a sense of accomplishment!

❑ **Stick to it**. If you have prepared properly, this shouldn't be all that difficult. However, there are always times where something derails your agenda and you need to pause and figure out which way to turn. While it may seem that many of the scenarios that pop up to derail our agenda are beyond your control (e.g. the room is hot and stuffy, a key person is out sick, the A/V isn't working, everyone is tired on a Friday, etc.), the truth is, how we respond to these difficulties is what separates a good-enough facilitator from an outstanding facilitator.

❑ **Use the agenda to put it all together.** As I plan out my agendas, I like to think of each engagement as consisting of four stages. These usually proceed in the following order:

1. Set the context. This helps everyone in the room answer the question: Why are we here? As you read through the rest of the book, look for activities and ideas to help you shed light on this question right from the get-go, and plan to start your agenda with ample time to address this question.

2. Share ideas and information. Once you have set the context, the next part of your agenda will most likely focus on sharing and growing knowledge collectively. Whether it's brainstorming ideas for your upcoming fundraiser, or learning a new technique for tackling a particular workplace challenge, this section is usually pretty action-packed.

Some questions to ask yourself while planning this portion might include:

> → What information do we need to cover?
> → Which method(s) would be the most fun and productive to cover that material?
> → How many different topics are we realistically able to cover?
> → How can I vary the activities we do to keep conversations flowing and allow for breathing in and out?

3. Synthesize what was covered

During the synthesis phase of your agenda, introduce an activity (or two) from the book that will allow participants to revisit the context you set at the beginning, and make direct connections between the purpose of the engagement, their experience, and everything that was covered thus far. Questions to ask yourself as you plan this section of the agenda include:

> → What questions can I ask participants to help them integrate what we have been covering?
> → How can this portion of the agenda help participants see new practices for themselves?
> → What activities could I use that would help participants connect both to each other - and to their thoughts about how this engagement has been useful to them?

4. Provide Closure

It is all too common for engagements to "run out of time" for the very important step of providing closure. All of the ideas in Section Five can be used to help participants feel closure. This includes planning next steps, completing evaluations of the session, and doing a closing "Think-Pair-Share."

Things to think about as you creating the closure portion of your agenda include:

> → What form of closure will participants most appreciate?
> → What can I do here to capture next steps and help participants leave on a productive and positive note?
> → What type of closure activities will help me, as the facilitator?

The chapters in this book will give you many ideas to help you put your agenda-puzzle together.

❏ **If you don't have "enough" time to start with, change your outcomes/expectations.** The first thing that usually happens with regards to timing, is that the timeframe for the engagement is set, either by you or by the group asking you to facilitate. By this I mean that either you say, "I need two hours for this workshop," or, you are told, "You have 30 minutes to run this conversation." While you may wish to have more than thirty minutes to run the conversation, it now becomes your job to figure out what you could do in thirty minutes to successfully run it. This is within your control. If you don't feel that the goal of having that conversation can be reached in thirty minutes, NOW is the time to discuss that with someone who has control over it. Either you need to adjust the outcomes and expectations or you need to adjust the time.

❏ **Be realistic about how much can be accomplished within your timeframe; don't try to do too much.** Long before you step into the room, you need to think about what is realistic given the time constraints. Time management often goes awry when facilitators try to fit too much within the time allotted. One of my least favorite pieces of feedback from participants is, "I wish we had more time," because to me this comment doesn't speak to the person wanting more of what I have to offer, it speaks to me trying to offer too much. If you only have 30 minutes, you really only have time to do a brief welcoming, one activity (e.g. make one decision, review one data set, introduce one new resource), and a short close-out/reflection. That's it.

If you are new to facilitating, it will take some trial and error to learn how much time things take, and it can vary greatly depending on variables like the number of participants and how much energy they happen to have on the day of the meeting. My one piece of advice here, if you are unsure of how much time to allot, is to leave more than you think! It is always better to end early, than to run overtime.

❑ **Practice, take notes, and reflect after your engagement.** If you are lucky enough to have the full two hours that you asked for in the example above, you have much more wiggle room. Particularly if it is a workshop or type of engagement you have run before, you probably now have a sense of what can be comfortably accomplished within that time frame. The key here is practice. I encourage you to take notes as you run sections of your agenda: Did this one need five more minutes? Did that one end ten minutes earlier than you thought it would? After the event, reflect on what helped you stay within your timeframe or what made it hard to stay within the allotted time.

I often run the same agenda multiple times, (i.e. when I am leading workshops). Depending on that particular group on that particular day, my timing may suddenly seem way off on an agenda that has worked many times before. Don't panic! Keep reflecting and practicing and you will start to notice patterns that will help you pivot and adjust in these situations. For example, if your first activity runs over time, when it usually fits perfectly within the timeframe you've allowed, you may realize you have a particularly chatty group. In this example, I might switch to written reflections (instead of conversations) for the rest of the agenda, to help minimize the excess talking.

❑ **Leave enough time for conversations and use a timer.** One thing I have really had to work on over the years related to this is leaving more time for pair/share and small group discussions, as I was often getting feedback that there was not enough time to talk. I realized that letting people talk, while a deep root of my Trans-

formational Facilitation philosophy, often made me uneasy because I was worried people would run out of things to say (and get bored), or get off topic. If this is true for you, I suggest setting a timer or really marking the clock during these periods of your agenda, so that you are not tempted to cut the conversations off early, because sometimes 3 minutes of this discomfort can feel like 10 minutes. You might also want to prepare a few extra questions or prompts for those who race through the conversation and are looking like they might start checking their phones, or walk around and engage people who look done to see what they came up with.

Along those lines, if you take away nothing else from this list, take this away: do not be afraid to use a timer! I do it all the time and it really, truly helps with keeping everyone on track. You can simply say, "I am setting a one-minute timer that will ring when your time is up," on a go-around, for example. Of course, you will still have a handful of people who continue talking after the timer chimes, but it really helps participants self-monitor, and you no longer have to feel anxious about cutting anyone off!

❑ **Leave yourself a cushion.** Lastly, if you are unsure of how much time to leave for any part of your agenda, add an extra 5-10 minutes to each piece of your outline. It is better to have leftover time at the end to work with (let people leave early, they love this!), than having to rush through or cut out pieces on the fly. I also find it helpful to think through how many people will be in attendance and do some mental math. If you are doing a pair/share where each pair will share, and you know you will have 20 people in the room, then you need to leave at least 15 minutes for the share out. Write down the exact times for each agenda item, then stick to them!

If timing is something that really is a struggle for you, I have included a "Think Sheet" on the next page that addresses a few key tips to managing your time more effectively.

NOTES

Time "Think Sheet"

How often have you left a meeting, workshop, or event, feeling either like it was a total waste of time, or that what was covered could have been done in five minutes, instead of two hours? There really is nothing that gets me more upset than when I feel like my time was wasted.

Why does that bother me so much? It's fair to say that, for most of us, time always seems to be in short supply. I used to joke that I needed a necklace like Hermione Granger's from the Harry Potter series. She uses it to take two classes that are happening simultaneously; she attends one class, then turns back time so she can go attend the other class. I relate all too well to this. So much to do, so little time.

As a Transformational Facilitator, time is your most valuable resource. When you have a group of people in front of you, whether they are your colleagues, staff, volunteers, or students, every minute needs to count. I like to think of each of the meetings, workshops, or events that I run as a smooth piece of music that flows rhythmically from one movement to the next. Each measure is important. The meter is important. The tempo is important. And it is of the utmost importance that participants are part of the orchestra, because, above all, their time (and their rhythm!) is important.

So here are a few suggestions for how a transformative facilitator can begin making better use of every moment that you have together with participants. I am sure you can think of even more ideas. Please feel free to share them, so we can all learn together.

❑ **Start on time.** I know this sounds obvious, but it is very easy to fall into the bad habit of waiting for "just one more person" before you start. Don't do it. Set the precedent that you will start on time. State it in your event reminder. Encourage people to arrive early to get settled in. Create a buffer by inviting everyone to a 15-minute snack and/or socializing time prior to the event for people to get those things out of the way so that you can start at the actual start time. When you start late, you are sending the message to the people who WERE on time that their time is not precious, or is less important than accommodating late-comers. Instead, encourage participants to welcome new people in as they arrive, and catch them up on what they missed.

❑ **End on time.** Better yet, end a few minutes early and "give back" a few minutes of everyone's day to them. That extra few minutes of space can feel like a fresh breeze or little ray of light, especially if you are working with highly-stressed and over-scheduled participants. Plus, it allows people to feel at ease to take their time packing up and chatting with each other before they leave. Try it, you'll be amazed at the positive environment it creates.

❑ **Use your time together for things that require being together.** Announcements, updates, information sharing - these are all better left in print, either as handouts or via email prior to the engagement. If the sharing itself does not require everyone being in the room together, then rethink whether you should spend your precious time together rattling off statistics or reviewing important dates. Instead, focus on activities that require interaction: conversations, brainstorming, reactions, questions, feedback, etc. Remember, your goal as a Transformational Facilitator is to keep your own voice to a minimum and encourage the voices of participants to take center stage. As you plan your agenda, ask yourself how you can cut yourself out of the agenda (e.g. by minimizing announcements from you), and where you can expand the time for participant voices to fill the room.

If you are concerned that people will not read memos or written updates, allow a few minutes during the engagement for people to read through a document that contains the announcements. You can even leave some time for people to ask questions about any of the updates or information. Depending on how urgent the question is, you can either answer it on the spot, or make a note of it and let people know you will address the questions in a later communication. Handling information-sharing in this way frees up your together time for inter-activity.

❑ **Leave enough time.** This is a big one for me and that I address above when thinking about crafting your agenda. When I open up a topic for conversation, and then don't leave enough time for participants to grapple deeply with it, it is because I hold a fear that people will run out of ideas and get bored or go off-topic. The more I facilitate, the more I have learned to let people get beyond their first idea by scheduling longer times for conversations, so they can move from just answering a prompt to actual authentic dialogue. One way I address my fear of the "early finishers" is by preparing additional topics or questions that I can share with participants who finish their conversations earlier than others. I have also learned to ask people how many more minutes they need (show of fingers), to help my orchestra set the pace.

❑ **Be present and attentive, and encourage others to do the same**. Express your gratitude for the time people are entrusting to you. Spend a few minutes at the beginning of the session creating agreements about how you will use your time together (see Chapter 22 for a fuller description): Will you allow people to use their cell phones, or do you ask people to turn them off and put them away? Do you want people to be mindful of their "air time," (meaning, if they've already shared, encouraging them to step back and allow other voices to be heard)? Will you offer breaks at a set time, or are people free to come and go as they need? Stating that time is valuable, that you value theirs, and that you expect everyone in the room to value each other's in these ways can help people focus so that everyone gets the most out of being present together.

What other ways can you think of to honor time and its worth?

_____

_____

_____

My task for you in this Think Sheet is to keep an eye on time, notice how people use it, (especially facilitated time), and create an action step for yourself about what you will do to improve your use of time.

CHAPTER 5
Use Visuals

I recently ran a workshop that involved a lot of moving parts—I wanted participants to walk away with three very distinct but interconnected pieces of knowledge. I was worried that we were packing too much "information" into one workshop, and that the various terms and systems we were introducing would get all jumbled up, like the way hot fudge melts hot fudge melts ice cream and makes a soupy slosh in the bottom of your bowl, (delicious, but no longer a set of distinct ingredients).

Enter: Visuals.

As I outline in the next chapter, I have pretty strong opinions about using PowerPoint, because I have mostly seen it used as notes for the presenter/facilitator, rather than as something truly additive and digestible for participants. The font is generally too small, there are too many words, there are too many slides. I often feel like the person in the front of the room is hiding behind the projections, as in, "Look at the wall, not at my face." And then there's the problem that it creates *a front of the room*, which is something a Transformational Facilitator is trying to eradicate. We can't be equals when we're all facing one direction.

I also know, however, that all learners, whether categorized as "visual" or not, benefit from seeing graphic or text representations of what they are talking and learning about because our ears can only grab on to so much. I was originally planning to create posters, but then realized that people might want to take the graphics home with them, so, trees forgive me, I provided handouts.

As you work to improve your Transformational Facilitation skills, one thing you may want to tackle is incorporating better visuals into your next meeting, class, or workshop. Here are the key elements that I find important to consider that may be helpful to you:

❑ **Keep it short.** As with my PowerPoint complaints which you will soon read, handouts that have too small a font, too many words, or just too many pages are much harder to digest than one clean sheet with a couple of bullets in (at least) 20-point font.

❑ **Keep it clean.** Unless you're a terrific graphic artist who really knows what you're doing, just use one sans serif font. That's it. One font. If you need to, go ahead and bold a few key words, or underline a particularly important phrase, but try to refrain from fancying up your text for no real reason.

❑ **Make sure it's legible.** When I was creating a visual recently, I printed it out only to realize that the contrast on the chart I had included was way too dark. I actually attended a workshop where the facilitator apologized for giving us handouts that I literally could not read. What's the point? Test your handouts before running 100 copies. The trees, and your participants, will thank you.

❑ **Include headers and footers.** A month from now, when a participant is cleaning up their desk and stumbles across your handout out of context, having a URL or the title of the workshop on each page of your handouts will help remind everyone where this material came from.

❑ **Distribute visuals one at a time**. I know it seems easier (and it is!) to staple together a big packet or stuff a folder and hand it out to participants right in the beginning of your engagement. But lately I have been experimenting with handing the sheets out one at a time, as we need them. I think there's something in the freshness of receiving a new sheet that perks people up and gets them excited about the material, with the added benefit that, since they can't be jumping ahead, it helps keep them focused on the one that is in front of them and is the topic of the moment.

By the way, the same is true here of visuals on the wall (or PowerPoint, for that matter). Keep un-introduced visuals covered until it is time to use them.

❑ **Make handouts interactive**. Have you noticed the interactivity in this book? In Chapter 7, I talk about this extensively, but for now, whether it's leaving space for notes, creating areas to fill in or respond to questions, or allowing large enough margins for doodling, anything you can do to help the participant co-create and own the page is a step closer towards being Transformational.

There are actually a lot of great books and resources on using visuals in facilitation, including graphic facilitation and using visuals in the design of the facilitation, which is what my Spark Decks do. If you're up for the challenge, take some time in the next few days to rethink how you are creating and using visuals with participants. How can you tweak what you are providing to make your materials even more clear and useful?

NOTES

CHAPTER 6
Use (or Don't Use) PowerPoint

I know we're only on Chapter 6, but it is time for me to address Powerpoint straight on. If you've been to a workshop or meeting with me in the past five years, you will know: I don't use it. So let me get the "why" behind that out of the way before I talk about how a Transformational Facilitator *could* use it, if you still decide want to go that route" with "if you decide you still want to go that route.

Reason #1: Something pretty much *always* goes wrong. This is just a basic fact of life that I'd rather not have to deal with. No matter how many times I see facilitators checking their slides, their connections, etc., at least one out of every five presentations (total estimate here) I've been to in the past year that involved a projected presentation had some sort of glitch that became super stressful for the facilitator.

Reason #2: I don't feel I need it. When I decided to stop using slides in my workshops because of the above-mentioned reason, I didn't miss it. In fact, I realized **I had been using it as a crutch**, which is my biggest complaint about how facilitators tend to use it. As I look back at old presentations, I find myself asking, "Did I really need to share that up on a big screen, or were there other ways and methods of communicating the same information?" Turns out, there were plenty of other ways.

Reason #3: MOST IMPORTANTLY, once you set up a screen and a projector, you've set up a focal point in the room, which I refer to as, if you can believe it, "the front of the room." In Transformational Facilitation, one of the goals is to eliminate this front of the room, because with a front created, you are reverting to one person standing there, up front, telling the rest of us how things ought to be. And the facilitator is pretty much always the only person who contributed to the creation of the Powerpoint presentation displayed there up front, so it is not in the the least bit participatory or conducive to active learning.

So those are my reasons. However, I know some of you are still going to continue to use PowerPoint, What I offer here are some things to think about as you design your presentation, so that it is Transformational Tool for learning and growing, rather than simply a bright tome of information.

❏ **Keep the words to a minimum.** There isn't anything that frustrates me more than a slide that is so crowded I can't even read the text. For inspiration, check out the Pechakucha website, www.pechakucha.com.

❏ **Think deeply about which few words you *will* use.** Maybe the slide just has one word, the key word you want people to discuss at that moment. A little anchor in a sea of ideas.

❏ **Better yet, just show an image.** I have always liked the idea of replacing words with images on a PowerPoint. It leaves so much more room for interpretation. Yes, this would certainly take more time and energy and thought on your part as facilitator, but even in searching for an appropriate image I think you will find you gain a deeper understanding of what you mean by the word you have selected.

❏ **Provide handouts.** If you need to provide participants with more text than a few words on a slide, give the text to them as a handout, with space for them to take notes and write rather than putting all of that text up on a screen where only those with excellent vision will be able to properly read it.

❑ **Email the documents.** On the topic of handouts, I often see people taking photos of slides that they want to remember. While this use of technology is certainly laudable, it is not exactly practical. Email the presentation to participants (save a tree!), or, if that isn't possible, provide copies, at least of key slides.

❑ **Keep it interactive.** I often see people putting up quotes, statistics, or graphs on a slide and asking participants to look at the slides and discuss what they see, and what it means to them, what it could mean for the topic at hand. I approve of this usage! At this point, you are truly using Powerpoint as an interactive tool for learning, not just a presentation.

❑ **Be mindful of your animations.** When those go glitchy, text bobs in and out of the screen, disappears too soon, becomes dizzying. Keep it simple.

❑ **Make sure you use your slides as signposts, not as a script.** I can think of nothing more tedious in a workshop or meeting than listening to someone read out their slides. (Sometimes even seeming surprised at what appears on the screen, like, "Oh, right, now I'm going to talk at you about this.") If you need a script, write a script, print it out, and keep it in front of you. I do!

Now that you've read this list of tips, here are a few reflection questions for you to ruminate on as you think about using PowerPoint.

What would be different about my event if I did not use a slideshow?

What could I do instead of a slideshow?

If I decide to move forward with using a slideshow, how will I keep it from taking my event off of its Transformational course?

CHAPTER 7
Create Handouts

By now, if you've been reading this book in order, you are probably already able to answer this question: What is something that all handouts from an event with a Transformational Facilitator have in common?

If you answered, "They are interactive," you are correct, and are picking up on the underlying foundation of what makes Transformational Facilitation what it is - anything but passive.

If this is not totally clear to you yet, if you are wondering what I mean by making your handouts "interactive," if you are confused about what that could look like, not to worry! That's what this chapter is all about.

❑ **Leave room.** At the most basic level, "interactive" means leaving space on the handouts for people

to take notes. This one is pretty easy. If you're using a PowerPoint, for example, you could simply print out the slides in the notes format, and voilà, done! But, because you're a Transformational Facilitator, there's a good chance you are not using a PowerPoint. So maybe it looks like printing out an agenda that has space beneath each item for participants to take notes. Or even just blank sheets of note paper with the word "Notes" at the top. It's a start.

❑ **Invite response.** At a slightly more intentional level, interactivity might look more like an exam or workbook. It might have questions that you plan to ask participants in, say, a pair-share, pre-printed along with thought or caption bubbles meant for participants to write responses in, as in this example.

What question
do you and
your partner
want to ask?

What is one new
idea you want to
share with
the group?

The idea is that the handouts are not just informative, but invite participants to respond to them. They become a facilitative tool, rather than just a set of agenda items, lists, or data. Perhaps most importantly, they are just as much created by the participant, as they are by you as the facilitator. If you put in time to create them, then let participants have equal amounts of time to create their share.

☐ **Get creative.** Handouts don't always need to be a piece of paper. If you are trying to spare the environment, these could, of course, be online, which can offer an even higher level of inter-activity, as in multiple people chiming in on a shared online document simultaneously. And even when they are on or made of paper, they don't have to be flat. They can (and should!) be

> → Various shapes
> → Different sizes
> → Made out of different types of paper (e.g. different thicknesses)

I try to switch it up - half sheets on cardstock, a bright pink sheet, a little booklet. How about using a postcard?

At this point you may be wondering why inter-activity is so important in Transformative Facilitation that I am telling you to even make your handouts interactive. Why does it matter whether people have a place to write down their thoughts? Why is the page asking questions? Why is this book constantly inviting responses?

The simple answer here is because all tools, (in this case handouts), at an event that is aiming to be Transformational must be Transformational from all angles, at all times. Every participant should be fully engaged for as much time as is possible during the session. This does not just include things happening temporally during the session. It also includes the collateral parts of the session that support participants. Like handouts.

Handouts are something I, myself, am still working on improving in my own work, even in this book. Making them look good, inviting as much creativity as possible (drawing space!), making them truly feel like they are not just a piece of paper, but a living, breathing document that is integral to the session content and participants' experience of it - that is what I am always thinking about as I prepare my handouts.

So here's my challenge to you for this chapter: The next time you are planning a workshop, event, or meeting, take a few extra minutes to think more creatively about the handouts you will distribute.

What handouts do I already distribute? Are they interactive?

_____

_____

_____

What can I do to make them more interactive, useful, and meaningful?

_____

_____

_____

In what places during my agenda can the handout truly become part of the learning?

_____

_____

_____

CHAPTER 8
Schedule Breaks

I'm always trying to keep my events break-free because my fear is that once people have a chance to float away to the restroom, snacks, or their cell phones, they will struggle to regain the focus and energy that they had before the break. My tendency is to simply tell people to take a break whenever they need one during the engagement, rather than scheduling it in. In fact, instead of offering an official break, I aim to vary the activities we do during our time together so that there are natural in-breaths and out-breaths. So that people are getting up and moving around periodically. So that there is a balance between quiet reflection time and noisy discussion time, between laser focus and big sky dreaming.

But I also know that at a certain point, people tend to get tired. If you haven't let them out for some fresh air, if they have a burning nag to check their email, if there's a quick call they have to make, then a break really is essential. So my rule of thumb is that if the engagement is more than 2 hours long, schedule a break.

In order to curb some of my nervousness around the loss of focus that can occur during a break, I like to give a little to-do during the break time. As in, "Go ahead and take a ten-minute break, and when you come back, be ready to share out your thoughts on the topic you were just discussing at your tables." Or, "Take fifteen minutes for a break, and while you are out, think about what questions you still have about our last activity."

As I write this, I imagine some of you groaning, "But people need to really just have a full on break!" And I believe you. They do. But what I'd like

to encourage you to think about here is what they need a break from.

> → Have you been making them think too hard for too long?
> → Sit too long?
> → Listen too long?
> → Have you covered so much information or made so much noise that they need a chance to be alone?

Because I actually believe that if you've crafted your agenda with this in mind, you can prevent people from feeling overwhelmed and fatigued. In fact, the time will absolutely fly.

So this is the challenge for this chapter: As you plan your agendas, think about how you can create enough of an ebb and flow that a short break, with a little "homework" assigned within that break, will be enough for everyone, so that they can still feel at ease to use the restroom and check their phones without the fear of missing something, but will also still be quietly attached to the content you've been covering.

If you are baffled as to what I am talking about with all the "ebb and flow," skip ahead to Section 4, which is where I offer ideas for supporting active learning that keeps people moving around and invigorated. I have seen these fun methods keep people engaged and energized, and mitigate the necessity for extensive breaks.

If you're ready for more about being prepared, let's move to the next chapter to talk about ambience.

NOTES

CHAPTER 9
Plan for Relaxation and Ease

Here are some of my thoughts on how ambience matters and how you can use your space to the best of its potential:

❑ **Choose a new spot.** Think about *where* you are holding your meetings and events and the environment you are creating by using that space. If you always hold your meetings or events in the same location, consider moving to a new room or heading offsite.

❑ **Tidy up.** Even if you cannot move your location, think about how you are using the space you have available to you. Take a minute to really notice the room. Are there messy papers lying around that you could clean up? A crooked blind you could straighten? Books you could stack on a shelf?

❑ **Reorganize the space.** Think about room flow. Is there an opportunity for people to easily move in and out, take a break, move their seat? I love moving tables and chairs around to make it more inviting. Here is my favorite set up.

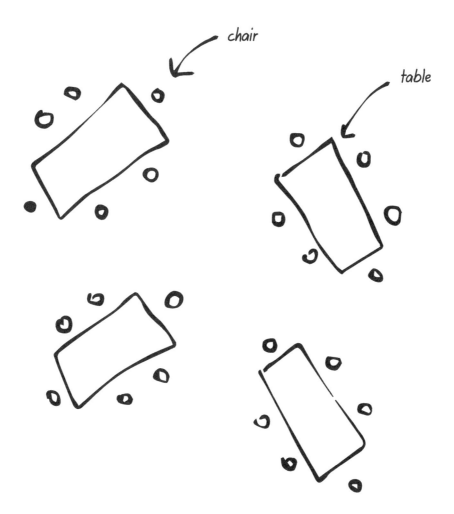

❑ **Beautify the environment.** Put flowers, seashells, or pretty tablecloths on the tables. Open the windows. Add a table lamp with a warm light bulb. Even small gestures like this can really warm up the environment and put people at ease.

❑ **Make it feel like a spa (or party!).** You may not be able to meet by the ocean or in the woods, but you can bring those things to you. Play the sounds of the sea or forest as people are entering the room. Generate a theme and make the event feel like a party by decorating within your theme and using metaphors from your theme in your agenda.

❑ **Offer better food.** If you can afford it, upgrade your snacks a little so people feel just that much more cared for than usual. Some easy ideas include putting sliced lemons or mint into the water pitchers, using "fancier" bowls and serving platters (e.g. from the dollar store), or bringing in a homemade treat.

This last point brings me to one of my favorite hospitality topics: food. Shortly after I moved to California, my best friend began dating a guy who was "into" food. This was a new concept to me, and, frankly, I found it unsettling. An apple was an apple. A boiled ravioli was no better or worse than a freshly made one. Iceberg lettuce was a fine salad. I used to make fun of the hours he would spend going to the farmers' market to get just the right kind of chard, or hand-rolling pasta. Are you kidding me? Just boil a 99 cent package of spaghetti!

But something began to happen the longer I hung out with him (since they are still together - almost twenty years later!). I began to actually notice the difference between a good apple and, well, a not-so-good one. And, right along with that, I began to take an interest in cooking better food, and not just cooking for practicality. It started with a few new cookbooks, a few magazine subscriptions, and before I knew it, I was having people over regularly to try out my creations. I still have never made pasta, but I have definitely made a lot of homemade bread, sauces, and salads - both with and without iceberg lettuce.

It will come as no surprise to you then that I take a great joy in feeding the people who attend my workshops and meetings. In fact, two of my most horrific memories over the years of providing professional development/conference planning both revolve around lunch mishaps (namely, lunch not showing up on time). Not events running over time, people not showing up, or critical evaluation feedback. Nope. What I remember with shame are the times I left participants hungry.

Feeding people who are in your care while you are facilitating goes beyond the idea of simply showing hospitality. People, both psychologically and physiologically, need to be fed in order to concentrate on the material at hand. Hungry minds wander down to rumbling bellies. The energy that good food and refreshing drinks provide set everyone up to feel their best, and do their best work.

Here are my tips for nourishing participants. I encourage you to try one or all of these at your next meeting, workshop, class, or event and notice if you see a difference:

❑ **Ask participants in advance if they have any dietary restrictions** and then make sure you provide choices that offer something for everyone (e.g. vegetarian, vegan, gluten free, nut allergies, etc.)

❑ **Focus on bringing in snacks that are healthy and provide long-lasting energy.** Trade out chips, sodas, and candy for:

> → Veggie sticks with hummus or dip
> → Fresh fruits like bananas, tangerines, or fruit salad
> → Yogurt with granola
> → Trail mix with nuts (as long as you don't have any allergies), raisins, (and a few M&M's!)
> → Hard boiled eggs or cheese sticks
> → Lemon or cucumber water

❑ **Make the spread look appealing** by putting toothpicks in the fruit, adding colorful napkins, or including a sprig of mint on each tray.

❑ **Label all of the foods** so that people with allergies can choose accordingly.

❑ **Refresh the snacks and add new ones throughout the engagement** (e.g. put the trailmix out on the tables later in the day).

And the bonus benefit of feeding your participants well and creating a beautiful space to engage in: You get to enjoy it, too!

Ambience "Think Sheet"

Last year I had the honor of hosting a retreat at the gorgeous Westerbeke Ranch in Sonoma, California. This was an idea that my Spark Decks' business partner, Oscar, and I had come up with last spring: Could we take the workshop training-of-trainers model we had created, and make it even more meaningful and Transformative? Yes. We could.

For several years, Oscar and I offered a free training-of-trainers, where people could come and learn how to run our workshops (which are very hands-on, fun, and model all of the Transformational Facilitation practices in this book). That way they could bring them back to their staff wherever they worked - or help us out when we needed someone to step in for us.

One of the things that struck us was that at each of these training-of-trainer events we had incredible and highly experienced leaders and facilitators from all over the San Francisco Bay Area and beyond in attendance. How could we capitalize on the voices in the room to help them get to know each other better, thereby building a stronger team of youth-serving professionals? At the same time, how could we make the event more enjoyable and relaxing for everyone, including ourselves as facilitators of the event?

Since heading to Hawaii seemed overly ambitious for our first retreat, we decided to look at locations within a one- to two-hour drive of San Francisco. We looked at overnight options, as well as day-use options. One of the things we had learned from running our Self Care for Youth-Serving Professionals workshop so many times is that water and nature are ubiquitous themes for high quality relaxation.

Being near the ocean or a swimming pool became central. Good food, beautiful scenery, space to unwind and walk around... this is what we were looking for. Our past training-of-trainers events had been in local room-for-rent spaces. They were functional, but not inspiring. This was going to be different.

We surveyed past training-of-trainer participants and people who we thought might like to attend, and found out that the only way an overnight would work is if we could find a space where everyone could have their own room. As it turns out, many of the retreat centers nearby only offer shared rooms and single rooms are very expensive, if even available. We also asked our contacts whether a weekday or weekend would be easier (weekday!), and what a reasonable price range would be (that one really ran the gamut).

We then hit the road, visiting a number of wonderful spaces, including an AirBnB on a horse farm, before deciding that the Westerbeke was definitely the place for us. Pool, hot tub, farm-to-table meals (you really have no idea how delicious the food there is!!!!), open and airy meeting rooms, a meditation labyrinth, gardens and grounds where we could eat fruit off of the trees (figs!). This was definitely it. A little slice of paradise.

As we designed our agenda, we made as much use of all that the space had to offer as possible. What would be the point of hosting an event somewhere beautiful if we spent all day inside a meeting room? We held a scavenger hunt that asked pairs to find discussion prompts hidden in various locations around the venue. We encouraged people to move outside to tables under trees and on the deck during peer-coaching times. We ate lunch outside by the pool and had a long afternoon break so that people could jump in to do laps or soak in the hot tub.

Facilitating an all day event can be utterly exhausting. But I left Westerbeke feeling like I, myself, had been on a retreat.

NOTES

CHAPTER 10
Keep Hands Busy

One of the easiest things I've started doing to put participants at ease and make my workshops and meetings more fun and focused is so simple it's almost laughable. I bought a couple of little plastic bowls, put one on each table in the event space before we get started, and fill them with crayons and markers.

Nothing says "let's put our creativity hats on" like a big pile of art materials. And while we do actually use them in some of the activities during the sesion (I'm always incorporating at least one art-type activity in my events), most of the time participants just help themselves and start coloring things in on their agendas or notebooks, sometimes even before the session has started.

Here's the best part: research strongly shows that having things to fidget with can help participants stay focused![5]

Have you ever seen a child who has a little gadget whirling around between her fingers? There's a reason the fidget spinner craze has been such a craze. While they can be distracting, research clearly shows that appropriate use of fidget toys do actually help people stay on task and even help people who may be feeling anxious stay more calm. While my boxes of crayons and markers were an easy gateway for me, I have seen facilitators put out all sorts of items, usually in boxes on tables, for participants to play with.

Here is a list of some items you may want to include in a "fidget box" for participants. I prefer things that don't make noise or a mess, and that are fairly inexpensive, like:

- ❑ Pipe cleaners
- ❑ Small containers of playdough
- ❑ Smooth stones
- ❑ Koosh balls
- ❑ Rubix cubes
- ❑ Origami paper
- ❑ Slinkies
- ❑ Stress balls
- ❑ Legos
- ❑
- ❑

I also like items that can be incorporated into an activity later on - thereby serving double-duty. Legos, like markers and crayons, are a great example, as they can be used in all sorts of visualization and team-building activities.[6] Same with playdough. Here are a few examples of how you can incorporate these manipulatives into a workshop:

- ❑ **Use them in a team-building exercise**. Give each team the same number of bricks and then ask them to build the highest lego tower they can, using the fewest number of bricks that they can.

---

[5] (Karlesky and Isbister) and (Slater)
[6] Lego Serious Play offers training and ideas on how to use legos in your facilitation. Learn more at www.lego.com/en-us/seriousplay, or pick up a copy of (Kristiansen and Resmussen).

❏ **Let them help visualize concepts**. Invite participants to create a form out of playdough that is agitated. Now have them rework the playdough so it represents calm. Now invite them to discuss with a partner how they, personally, make the shift at work from agitated to calm.

❏ **Use them to illustrate a point.** I recently invited participants to write down each of their work projects on an index card. I then asked them to create piles of Legos on each card that represented how much time/effort they spend on that project, using a different color Lego for each project. Next I asked them to create a tower where their lowest-priority projects were at the bottom, and highest-priority projects at the top. Were they spending too much time on low-priority projects? (Yes! Many of them were and it was very eye-opening!)

❏ **Incorporate them into an icebreaker**. Ask them to choose one item from the bin that in some way represents them. Now ask them to find a partner, introduce themselves, and discuss why they chose that particular object.

❏ **Use them to pair people or create groups**. Ask everyone to choose a pipe cleaner. Now ask people to find someone who has the same color pipe cleaner. This person is now their partner for a discussion prompt or activity.

Here's another reason to provide fidget objects: If you don't, people will make their own. And I think someone squishing a Koosh ball is much easier to take as a facilitator than someone endlessly clicking their ballpoint pen, don't you?

NOTES

CHAPTER 11
Bring Extra Everything

Here's something they don't teach you in facilitation school: bring absolutely everything you and your participants need, even if it is something that may seem obvious, like pens.

I cannot tell you how many times I have asked participants, "Who needs a pen?" prior to doing a writing activity halfway through a workshop or meeting, only to find out that a number of them have spent the entire first half of the meeting without one.

Here's my solution: make yourself the facilitator's equivalent of a first aid kit! Here is what I have and recommend for the "kit" I bring to every engagement:

❑ **Pens.** For the reason just stated above. In fact, I buy a lot of pens and then let participants know they can keep them if they want to.

❑ **Dry Erase Markers.** There is often a whiteboard in the rooms I find myself in (classrooms, boardrooms, etc.), but there is almost never the markers to go with it. I greatly prefer using a whiteboard to chart paper, when possible, because it saves trees.

❑ **Chart Paper Markers.** I always ask if there is a whiteboard in the rooms I will be in. If the answer is "no" I make sure to have chart paper. The important thing here is to make sure you don't use your chart paper markers, which are usually permanent, on a whiteboard, or your whiteboard markers, which will dry up quickly if used on paper, on the charts.

❑ **Blue Tape.** This is generally for hanging the chart paper, but can also be used to hang signs, or reinforce the stickiness of name tags or sticky notes that keep falling off.

❑ **Blank Paper.** This is for making signs. Sometimes I show up to a space and the room we are in is really hard to find. By the time participants have found the room, they are agitated, out of breath, and sometimes even late. A few well-placed arrows/signs can make a big difference in how much more calmly people show up.

❑ **Blank Name Tags.** I buy name tags in bulk and just keep them in my kit. It's just one less thing I have to remember as I am packing up my other workshop or meeting materials.

❑ **Sticky Notes.** As with name tags, I use these a lot so I buy them in bulk and always keep them with me.

❑ **Ibuprofen.** The only thing worse than facilitating with a headache, is facilitating while one of your participants has a headache. I give away more ibuprofen than I use myself because it really cheers people up when you are able to offer them relief.

❑ **A Phone Charger.** Like the ibuprofen, I am more often loaning this to participants than using it myself. I labeled it, too, so that it finds its way back to me at the end of the event.

❑ **PowerPoint Connector.** Similar to the phone charger and ibuprofen, since I don't often use

PowerPoint, this is really for my colleagues, especially when I'm coordinating an event, although I try to remind people to bring all of their own cords and connectors.

❑ **Thumb Drive**. While most people house their documents, presentations, and videos online, it never fails that at some point the internet will not work well and these critical elements cannot be accessed. I encourage my colleagues to put everything they need onto a drive "just in case," but because sometimes they don't listen, I bring one so they can transfer materials from their personal computers to the venue computers if the internet isn't working properly.

❑ **A Large Clip-on Flower**. Because I coordinate and host a lot of events, having an identifier on me can help participants find me in a crowd. I let everyone who is helping with the event know that if someone runs into a problem or has a questions, they should look for the "woman with the bright orange flower in her hair."

Of course, you can also put all of the other "essential" items that you would put into any other emergency-type kit into your bag, particularly if you will be facilitating in different locations each day, which is usually true for me. Those things might include feminine products, tissues, needle and thread, earplugs, water bottle, etc. You may find yourself often sharing these things rather than using them yourself, but as a Transformational Facilitator, being prepared to meet participants' needs doesn't always just mean having a tight agenda.

Use this space to brainstorm what you might want to include in your "kit" and then go ahead and build it!

SECTION TWO
CREATE A SAFER ENVIRONMENT

Everything that a Transformational Facilitator does is working toward creating an environment that feels inclusive, encourages engagement, and brings out openness in participants. This is not easy, especially since so many of us walk into engagements carrying all of the history of our past experiences with this group, this topic, this format, this setting, etc. Institutional hierarchy, racial dynamics, sexism, and many other manifestations of power and privilege make their way into engagements, regardless of how warm, open, and prepared you are.

I love the analogy of a closed fist from Dan Siegel.[7] When we are feeling calm and safe, it is like our hand is in a fist; our fingers are the rational part of our brain, that is ready to think, learn, and engage, keeping our emotions in check. When we are not feeling calm and safe, our fingers fly up, creating an open palm and exposing that part of our brain, (the amygdala, for you science buffs), that triggers our fight-or-flight response. It is impossible to openly engage or learn when we are in that agitated state, and this is why paying attention to the environment matters to a Transformational Facilitator.

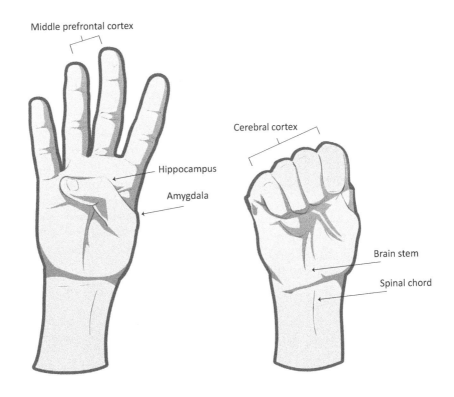

Middle prefrontal cortex

Hippocampus

Amygdala

Cerebral cortex

Brain stem

Spinal chord

Hand model after Dan Siegal.

7 (Siegal)

If you aim to accomplish nothing else as a Transformational Facilitator, I encourage you to at least set your sights on creating a welcoming, responsive environment for participants, in any small ways you can. This might include any and all of the following:

- ❑ Making sure your space is accessible for people with mobility issues
- ❑ Being mindful of people who enter the space visibly agitated and asking if there is anything you can do to support them
- ❑ Providing materials and/or translation into relevant languages as needed
- ❑ Publically acknowledging power dynamics either amongst participants, or between yourself and the group
- ❑
- ❑
- ❑

Originally, as I was writing this book, this section was focused on creating a *safe* space. Through many revisions and a lot of feedback, I realized that it is impossible to create a space that is truly safe, and, in fact, striving for safety can sometimes inhibit our ability to do things like push ourselves to try something new, or provide critical but meaningful feedback. The following section, therefore, walks you through steps you can take to make your engagement truly welcoming and *safer*, so that people can show up as their best selves, take risks, do their best work, and positively, fully, and wholeheartedly contribute to the event.

On many levels, this particular section also focuses on your role, as the Transformational Facilitator, in making this happen. This may mean checking your own agitation level, paying attention to the mood of the group, and being mindful of comments or questions that arise that may be hurtful or dismissive of others in the room. There is no place that you are a greater role model than in developing a safer, braver, more inclusive environment. If you, yourself, are not feeling welcomed, courageous, and safe, neither are participants. Before you dive in to this section, take a moment to reflect on the following questions:

What makes me feel safer, willing to take risks, or valued in a meeting, class, workshop, or event?

_____

_____

_____

What makes me feel unsafe, undervalued, or unwilling to take risks in a meeting, class, workshop, or event?

_____

_____

_____

In what ways do I already help the people around me feel safer, valued, and willing to take risks?

_____

_____

CHAPTER 12
Facilitate Warmth

A recent study published by researchers at Harvard shows that "parental warmth" has a positive impact on people's well-being in adulthood.[8] While this may seem self-evident, it is interesting to see the research that backs up an assumption many of us make - that positive child-adult interactions early in life contribute to positive outcomes later in life.

Those of you who work with children and youth will recognize this immediately as an underlying tenet of both Youth Development and Social and Emotional Learning practices. These frameworks explicitly aim to create warm, caring environments in schools and youth programs. Simple practices like knowing every student's name, saying "Hello, I'm glad you're here" to each child you greet, or making time to welcome your whole group at the beginning of your time together through a game or song are just a few of the many ways I have seen this done.

But it is still not happening everywhere. This is where Transformational Facilitation comes in: The only way to ensure that staff and parents/caregivers are creating warm environments for their students and children, or that our employees are welcoming customers, or that colleagues are acting civil to each other, is to model that warmth in our interactions with them as supervisors and facilitators.

That is my challenge to you with this chapter. Make it your practice to do some or all of the following at your next staff meeting, class, or engagement, knowing that this modeling has the power to affect

the way participants, in turn, interact with clients, students, and customers - and each other.

If you find it difficult to be extroverted, pick something from the list that will feel warm to participants, but that also feels comfortable to you. I have seen very introverted facilitators do an incredible job of making people feel welcomed, without running up to everyone with a booming voice and a backslap of welcome.

❑ **Say "Hello."** Make an effort to introduce yourself to anyone you don't know who enters the meeting or engagement (by the way, you can do this even if you are not the facilitator!). Ask a few questions like their name, where they work, who they work with, why they showed up here today, etc. Spend as much time as you can getting to know who is in the room, then use people's names and any information you know about them throughout the engagement. The key idea is *"I'm glad you're you and I'm glad you're here."*

❑ **Smile**. You may not have time to introduce yourself fully to each person, but you can at least acknowledge their presence through a smile and nod. Aim to be set up and ready before people start arriving so that when they step through the door you are able to be present and show them that *"I see you and you make me happy."* Throughout the engagement, notice your facial

8 (Chen et al.)

expressions. Are you radiating that smile still, or has it capitulated into a frown?

❑ **Let them share.** Before launching into "business," allow time for people to welcome and share with each other. For example, you can have them each share one way they help people feel welcomed, or a way they show kindness or caring for their children or the youth they work with. The main purpose here is to exchange on ideas on how we communicate "*I am here to support you.*"

❑ **Notice your body language.** For example, keep your arms by your sides, uncrossed; face people fully when they are speaking; stand in front of any podium or table that is between you and participants; put your phone away and look up instead; and nod as people are speaking to acknowledge you are hearing them. Our body language communicates, "*Your presence is important to me and puts me at ease.*"

❑ **Provide positive feedback.** Laugh with people; support their comments with a "Yes!" "Exactly," or "Thank you for sharing that important thought;" or even hand out raffle tickets, stickers, or prizes when people share their opinions to keep it fun and project, "*I connect with your thoughts and ideas and they matter to me.*"

❑ **Be yourself.** If you are feeling nervous, it's fine to let that show, you're human! Being authentic and making your vulnerability transparent will not only increase trust between you and participants, it is also modeling that behavior and will encourage others to be authentic and promote trust amongst attendees.

Here is a reflection to help you envision what this might look like.

Who is the most warm and welcoming person you know? What about that person makes you feel at ease? What attributes about that person could you authentically emulate that might help you seem more open and welcoming to participants?

_____

_____

_____

How do different cultures express welcoming? What cultural difference could effect how welcomed your participants feel?

_____

_____

_____

What physical spaces make you feel welcomed? What about the physical environment helps you feel welcomed? How can you emulate this for participants?

_____

_____

_____

CHAPTER 13
Post a "Do Now"

A "Do Now" activity is something that is written up on a PowerPoint, board, or chart paper as participants enter the room where the meeting, class, or engagement is being held. "Do Nows" serve a dual purpose: First, they give participants something to do other than checking their phones, which is what most people will default to when entering into a new (and, therefore, slightly uncomfortable) space. Secondly, they help participants warm up to the topic, or a sub-topic that will be covered during the meeting.

"Do Nows" are especially useful for events where people a) trickle in, b) people don't yet know each other, or c) there is a rather large group of people. These scenarios can make those events feel especially awkward for participants, and a "Do Now" can do wonders for helping them ease into the space. When I host large workshops that are open to people from many different agencies, I really love to use "Do Nows." While some people will naturally strike up a conversation with someone near them, or quietly peruse the agenda, most people will turn to their phones. This is not necessarily bad, but if you are trying to create a Transformative environment, you want to get people involved and engaged from the minute they walk through the door - and checking social media or answering emails and texts is the opposite of that goal.

For example, let's say you are hosting a back-to-school parent orientation where you will go over school rules, important dates, etc. As parents enter, there is a PowerPoint slide that reads:

> **Do Now:** Grab a snack. Find a seat. Turn to the people sitting near you, introduce yourself, and share your responses to any or all of the following questions, "What was your favorite part of going back to school when you were young? What was your least favorite part? As a parent, how do you feel about your child's return to school after the summer break?"

Or, imagine you are leading a meeting for your staff about new safety procedures for emergencies. As they enter the meeting room, there is a sentence on the board that reads:

> **Do Now:** Think of a time you were in an emergency situation. How were you prepared? How could you have been even better prepared? On the index cards provided, write down one "tip" you wish you had known prior to the emergency.

Once the meeting starts, you can use these "tips" as part of an icebreaker or other type of sharing activity. In fact, "Do Nows" often lead really nicely into opening icebreakers or personal introductions, so you may want to think more deeply about how you integrate the "Do Now" into the opening of the meeting.

Two things to keep in mind: The "Do Now" serves to both provide a constructive use of time (something people generally expect and appreciate when they come to a meeting), as well as to gently introduce the topic at hand. Note that If people don't immediately start in on it, make sure to point the "Do Now" out to them; if they have never seen one before, it won't be obvious to them that they are supposed to follow the instructions.

Here are a couple of further "Do Now" ideas for you to think about using the next time you host a meeting, class, or event, followed by some spaces for you to generate your own "Do Nows" for topics you will be presenting soon. Remember, tailor your questions or the activities to fit the topic(s) you are going to be covering. A "Do Now" should fore-shadow and frontload what is to come!

Do Now: Around the room you will find quotes about leadership. Find one that resonates with you and, using the pens and paper on your table, write down why you like that particular quote.

Do Now: Sign in and find a seat next to someone you don't already know. Introduce yourself and share why you decided to sign up for this class. What are you hoping to get out of being here?

Do Now: Using the sticky notes and markers on your table, write down three ideas (one per sticky note) for topics you would like to explore during our monthly staff development meetings this year.

Do Now: Turn to the person sitting next to you and share your favorite part of yesterday's workshop. What is one question about the topic that you still have? What are you looking forward to about today's workshop?

Use the blank "Do Now" squares to brainstorm some questions or activities you can use at your next engagement.

DO NOW:

DO NOW:

DO NOW:

DO NOW:

CHAPTER 14
Learn Names

What's in a name? One of my favorite opening discussion questions is an icebreaker that involves people sharing the story of their name with each other: the meaning, the family history, the cultural connections. Knowing and calling someone by their name (with proper pronounciation) is an important part of Transformational Facilitation. Why? Because it communicates the message to the person, "I see you as an individual of importance, not just an anonymous face in the crowd."

In fact, in Transformational Facilitation, knowing everyone's name is crucial. Unlike in a panel or lecture, where there is little to no engagement with or between participants, the highly participatory and interactive nature of events that adhere to the principles of Transformational Facilitation make knowing everyone's names critical. Not only does it foster trust and familiarity, it is also simply useful when calling on people, highlighting specific comments ("... as Sam said earlier..."), and connecting individuals to each other, ("Kris and José both understand...").

I cannot count the number of times I have heard people say, "I am terrible at remembering names." I think sometimes what people really mean is, "I am terrified that I am going to forget someone's name." What I see is that we don't forget the names of people we truly know and care about. I know, for myself, when I meet someone new, if I don't focus on what they say their name is, or attach it to other useful information about the person, it all goes in one ear and out the other. Literally five seconds after they've told me, I've forgotten what they said.

But when I create the conditions for remembering someone's name, it sticks. How can we set up our facilitation space so that the people in front of us are not just a bunch of anonymous faces that we have to label with a name, but are truly friends, whose names we would never forget?

Clearly this is easier said than done, so I offer a few suggestions here to help you and your participants get to know each other and really learn each other's names:

- ❑ **Let everyone create a name tag** that they wear throughout the engagement. This is especially helpful for us visual learners. Additionally, a practice that is increasing in popularity is to include the person's preferred pronoun (e.g. he/him, she/her, they/them).

- ❑ **Play a name game.** A quick internet search will pull up dozens. One of the quickest and easiest to run is to simply have people state their name and a word that starts with the same letter that describes them (or their feelings about the upcoming topic, or their favorite food, etc., e.g. My name is Eva and I am Energetic). While this may seem juvenile, people tend to genuinely enjoy these types of icebreakers. Follow the activity with a debrief discussion on why it is important to know and remember names, and allow people to share their tricks for remembering.

- ❑ **Let people share the story of their name.** As I mentioned earlier, this icebreaker is always interesting. After people have shared with a partner, let the partners introduce their new friend and retell the story they just heard.

❑ **Write the names down**. I do this at meetings when people are going around the table saying their name and where they work. I keep my little map handy so I can remember who each person is. Usually by the end of the meeting, my "cheat sheet" has helped me remember everyone's name.

❑ **Make nameplates**. Give people cardstock folded in half and either markers, or magazines/scissors/glue to create a nameplate that they display in front of where they are sitting. Allow people to share why they chose to display their name with those images. The visual elements are helpful in both learning more about the person and in remembering their names.

If this is something you feel you really need to work on, there are entire books written about this topic. Feel free to put this book down for a minute and go check one out from the library today.

NOTES

CHAPTER 15
Use an "Attention-Getting" Signal

For those of you reading this who come from the education world, an attention-getting signal is nothing new. It is simply a signal to your group that it is time to quiet down and listen to instructions. In fact, even if you don't consciously use an attention-getting signal (yet) in your engagements, you actually probably do use something, because even saying, "Alright everyone, it's time to wrap up your conversations," is a signal!

Remember, in events that are using Transformational Facilitation, rooms get noisy as people are often talking with each other in pairs or small groups. Shouting at people to get them to quiet down erodes the feeling of calm, ease, and safety you have so carefully constructed. With this in mind, here are some thoughts on how to get participants' attention during workshops and meetings in order to maintain an environment of peace and respect.

❑ **Pick a signal.** Personally, I like to use a silent raised hand. Participants are asked to also raise their hands when they see mine raised, spreading the signal all around the room, so that people who have their backs to me also see it. Some people I know like to use a little bell, or even clap, although I don't like the loud signals because people need a minute to finish their sentences, and a loud signal is disruptive. (In fact, best practice informed by trauma work notes that in communities where violence is prevalent, loud attention-getting claps can trigger PTSD responses, so it is a good idea to avoid loud signals, especially when working with youth or anyone involved in trauma.)

❑ **Teach the signal to your group.** One of the first things I do in my engagements is explain that it will be noisy at times and that we will be using a signal to bring everyone back together. I introduce my raised hand and then explain that when they see mine up, everyone else should raise their hand and finish their last thoughts.

❑ **Use it consistently.** If you are using a signal - use it! Don't default to the, "Alright everyone..." phrase. It can sometimes take a few seconds for everyone to quiet down, but it works. The more you use it, the more comfortable people will be, and the more quickly your room will settle down.

❑ **Wait until everyone has seen the signal and finished their conversations to begin talking yourself.** This is really important. People get off-task, lost, and frustrated when they can't hear clearly. Before you start speaking, listen for a second or two to make sure everyone is really quiet, that they've really finished what they were saying, and that they are looking at you ready to listen. I like to take a deep breath here, just to ensure the air is really clear.

❑ **Give them more time.** After you've used your signal, if it seems like people were really having a hard time wrapping up their conversations, you can ask if people need more time, and if so, to raise their hands with the number of additional minutes they would like. Using a signal means you are in charge of when people have to stop talking, but if they weren't ready to stop, honor that by giving them more time!

My attention-getting signal is well established, and people who have attended more than one of my workshops or meetings are already familiar and comfortable with it. If people seem to balk the first time you use a signal, stick with it! Soon it will feel like second nature to both you and participants, and you will find that your engagements flow much more smoothly when you are able to quickly and quietly get everyone's attention.

NOTES

CHAPTER 16
Play Music

When do you listen to music? In the car, while you're making dinner, during a workout? Music is a powerful tool that can help people relax, feel inspired, and overcome tedium or challenges (chopping all those onions!). In fact, research shows that music and our social capabilities are tied together.[9] So let's take a minute here to explore how you can use music in your facilitation to make your engagements even more welcoming and engaging!

The first, and easiest, way to incorporate the power of music into your events is simply by playing music at key points:

❑ **While people are entering the room.** I started doing this only about a year or so ago, but now, if for some reason I forget my music player and there isn't any music, I really feel the vacuum it leaves. Having music playing in the room as people enter just makes the room feel more welcoming.

❑ **During a mingling activity** while people are trying to find partners. Finding a partner or walking around in a room full of strangers can be a rather stressful activity for some people. Putting the music on helps everyone feel more upbeat as they move around the room looking for their match and triggers a "this is fun" response that eases tension. If you're lucky, you'll have a goofball who actually starts dancing during the mingle, which is really fun and lightens the mood.

❑ **While people are silently writing** and/or reflecting in pairs. Although some people find the music distracting, a quiet bit of inspiring music while people are writing or chatting with a partner can help put people into their creative zone and raise optimism about potential. Make sure you check in with participants to find out if anyone will find the music distracting. If so, keep the volume low, and/or move the source of music as far as possible from anyone who will find it distracting (so that they cannot hear it).

You can play around with the kind of music you play, too. For example, I have used a "superhero" playlist when I wanted people to feel really inspired, a space-themed playlist when I was running a retreat at a science/space center, and a relaxation-mix when I was running a self-care workshop. If you don't subscribe to a music service, YouTube has lots of free playlists that people have put together (just turn the volume down when an ad starts to play!).

The second way to incorporate music is by actually using it as part of an activity. For example,

❑ **In team builders.** A fun team builder is to print out the lyrics of a song and cut them into lines. Now play the song and let teams try to quickly put the lyrics back in order as the song plays. After the activity, reflect on what social-emotional skills everyone had to use to accomplish the activity.

---

[9] (Schulkin and Raglan)

❏ **To inspire reflection.** Play a song or verse/chorus of a song related to the topic you are covering. You can now ask participants to reflect on how the lyrics or song relates to their work, or the topic you are covering. Another option is to play two very different songs and ask them to discuss with a partner which one resonates more with them and why.

❏ **As an icebreaker.** Ask participants to choose a song that represents how they are feeling, and share it with a partner.

The final way to use music that I am encouraging here is to have participants create it. You can ask them to "write a piece" that describes the flow of their work day, for example. There are many ways to let participants compose:

❏ The easiest way is to have people **create beats** on their tables or laps. Have each table assign roles: one person keeps a steady beat, one person lays a steady but fancier beat on top of that one, one person adds flourishes, etc. Or, just let people free form as a table and see what they come up with!

❏ Bring in an assortment of "**things that make noise.**" Sticks, shakers, little flutes, whistles, pots and pans... let everyone choose something and create an orchestra. You can even choose someone to be the "conductor" with a pencil baton and let them direct who plays when, how loud, how fast, etc. Can you envision all of the reflection questions you could ask after doing this?! (Some examples could be, "How is our team like the orchestra we just created?" "What did you notice about how we reacted to the 'conductor' and how is this similar/dissimilar to our roles in this organization?" or "How did it feel to be part of making this music? What was easy about it? What was difficult? Why?")

❏ Although people are sometimes shy about **singing**, it can actually be a fun activity to all sing together. You can use a karaoke app, play the radio, or just do it acapella. Even if it's just singing "Happy Birthday" to someone in the room, singing has a great effect on people's mood and energy!

Of course, the many reflection options after the music-making are also key. "How did you feel while you were making music? How do you feel now that it is over? How did this relate to our topic of the day? How does this relate to your job?" This part is so much fun, and I think you will be pleasantly surprised by the depth and level of creativity that their responses hold!

Take a minute now to think about when, what, and how you might use music in your next engagement.

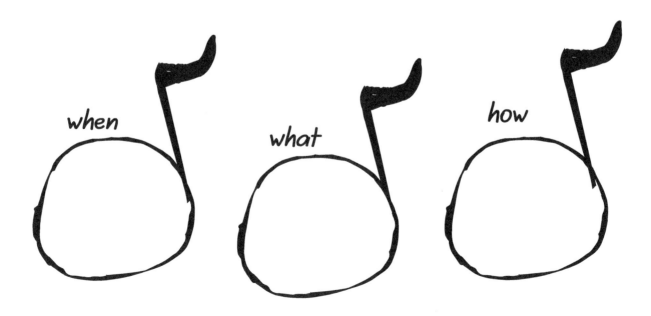

CHAPTER 17
Open with an Icebreaker

I know some of you might cringe at this, but I love icebreakers and would never start a meeting or workshop without one. No matter how well people know each other, they are entering your event space with a million things flying around in their heads, and often with a great deal of nervous energy, either from anticipation of your event, or from other things going on in their lives. Giving everyone a chance to literally warm up their bodies and minds by moving around, getting to know each other, and using their voices will help them immeasurably throughout the session. If you don't already do some kind of warm-up activity, today is the day to start!

Here are some ideas on how to make this happen:

☐ **Relate the icebreaker to the topic you will be covering.** For example, if our topic of the day is "staying organized," I might do an icebreaker that involves asking pairs to sort a bunch of random objects that I provide (e.g. a box of office supplies), and then explaining to another pair how their sorting system works. Or I may ask participants to discuss a series of questions like, "Which parts of your life feel organized, and which don't? What systems do you use to stay organized? What helps and motivates you to be organized?" etc. In teacher-speak, we call this opening activity "the hook," as it gets people excited and clear on what we will be covering during the engagement.

☐ **Encourage participants to move around and meet new people.** I love mingling activities because people have to walk around the room and have the opportunity to talk to several different partners. You can either play music and ask participants to find a partner; once the music stops, or you can ask them to find a specific partner, for example, someone who is wearing similar shoes to the ones they are wearing. Change partners at least three times, and each time give them a different discussion prompt (related to your topic!) to discuss after they have introduced themselves.

☐ **Keep it short.** Having everyone share to the whole group is probably not feasible if there are forty people in the room, but having them share in pairs or small groups definitely is! The goal does not have to be for everyone to meet everyone else, since they will hopefully have opportunities to meet more people at other points during the engagement. Instead, the goal should be for everyone to have an opportunity to get warmed up, whatever form that takes. I usually aim for twenty minutes, which feels like a great use of our time if it really launches us into our topic, which, when done well, it will!

☐ **Do introductions.** If you want to do introductions as part of your icebreaker, I like to have partners introduce each other, rather than introducing themselves. Why? Because some people struggle to keep things short, and others feel uncomfortable talking about themselves in front of a large group. Ask pairs to introduce themselves to each other (they can take notes if they feel nervous about remembering details), and then have the partners introduce each other to the group.

☐ **Look online or at your local bookstore for ideas.** There are so many icebreakers on the internet, you can even do a search for "icebreaker [your topic]" so that all of the work is done for you! I also often refer to a couple of different books[10] I have for ideas; all you need are one or two good ones to keep you in fun-icebreaker-mode for a long time.

❑ **Debrief the icebreaker after you are finished.** Some questions I like to ask participants to think, write, or discuss include:

> → Why do you think we opened with this activity?
> → How did you feel before/after?
> → How did this activity relate to today's topic?
> → How might you use this activity with staff or stakeholders in your work environment?

❑ **Keep it fun!** People actually learn and perform better when they are having a good time and are feeling relaxed! Set the tone for your engagement by keeping things light, funny, and upbeat. Especially if you are planning to cover a tough topic, starting out with a solid, fun icebreaker can really help keep people up.

Although it may seem like a waste of time to spend twenty minutes running around the room or playing a game, I actually cannot think of a better way to spend time during an engagement because opening this way will make the rest of your time together more productive, safe, and warm. Try it out and let me know if I'm wrong!

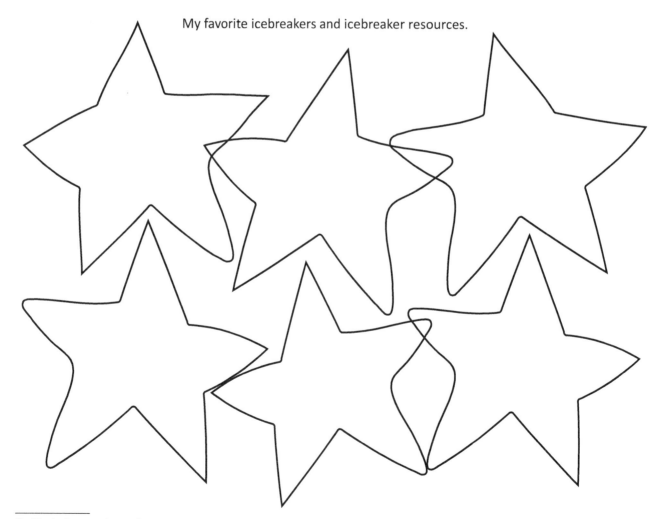

My favorite icebreakers and icebreaker resources.

---

[10] I like (Ashton and Varga), although I'm afraid it might be out of print. I have also enjoyed the activities in the SmartFun Activities Books series, especially the improv and drama games. Even though this series is designed to be used with children, I have found adults love the activities just as well.

Icebreaker "Think Sheet" - Visioning Perfection

I don't know how it is where *you* work, but staff burnout is a particular danger amongst people who work with youth (e.g., teachers, after-school staff, counselors, etc.). Because of this, I am often brought in to run a "Self Care" workshop that helps staff think deeply about how they are taking care of themselves, before they find themselves out with the flu or too tired and stressed to enjoy their job, let alone their lives. I learned a version of this opening activity that I use in that workshop from Courtney Pinkerton, a life coach and author of the book, *The Flourish Formula*.[11] While I have found it to be extremely useful and effective with educators, you will see that it can work with any group that could use a little time to de-stress and unwind. Before I explain the *why,* let me describe how the activity unfolds.

I start by turning up my spa playlist (there are many to be found on YouTube) and asking everyone in the room to push their chairs back, uncross their legs and put their feet flat on the floor while uncrossing their arms and resting their hands gently on their laps. I invite them to either close their eyes or quietly look down towards the floor. When everyone has shifted into this "unwound" position, I lead the group in taking three, slow, deep breaths - in through the nose, out through the mouth. I often turn off the lights.

I now invite participants to either return to a memory of, or envision a yet-to-occur, "Perfect Day." To guide them, I slowly ask the following questions:

> → Where are you?
> → Is it sunny, rainy, foggy?
> → Is it warm or cool?
> → Do you feel any breezes or warmth from the sun or a fireplace?
> → What smells do you notice?
> → What are you wearing? Blankets? A bathing suit?
> → What are you doing? Standing, sitting, moving, laying down?
> → Are you eating anything?
> → What sounds do you hear?
> → Who are you with? Or are you alone?

Lastly, I ask them to notice how they feel in their perfect day and to remember that feeling as they open their eyes and return to the room.

Next, I ask participants to quietly stand up and find a partner - someone they don't yet know. After introducing themselves, I ask them to share their perfect days and try to find three common elements between the two days. When they are finished, I ask each partner to find another set of partners, so that everyone is in a group of four. Between them, I challenge them to find two common elements. Depending on the group size and time, I may then ask the foursomes to find another group and see if they can find a common element amongst all eight of them.

I have done this activity dozens of times, and the same themes always emerge: water, nature, and

---

[11] (Pinkerton)

often, quiet. And I always point out that this is pretty much the opposite environment as the one that we, as educators, work in; we are mostly indoors, around concrete, in buildings where it is loud and busy.

As participants return to their seats, I ask them to think about why we opened our Self Care workshop with this activity. Why is it helpful to know, define, and remember our "Perfect Day?"

Of course, this is the key purpose of the activity: to understand that we all have a place where we are calm, relaxed, and happy. That if we can just take a minute to step out of the our actual environment, take a few deep breaths and return to that Perfect Day, we can release so much of the tension that WE DON'T EVEN REALIZE WE ARE CARRYING.

The meditation takes less than five minutes. But that brief escape has the power to help us recenter and ground ourselves as we return to the stress of our workday.

Last year, before I ran this meditation, the group had been working on creating timelines of the major milestones in their lives. Almost everyone in the room had a "What's Next" stone as their last step, as if the whole group were on the edge of launching into a new, but yet unknown, future.

After the meditation and sharing, one of the participants pointed out that he felt reconnected with his "What's Next" stone. That it helped him see where he should be heading... more time outdoors, more time with family, more time to breathe.

I invite you to do two things:

❑ First, I encourage you to try the Perfect Day meditation, either by yourself or with your staff. Open your next meeting with it! Notice if you can see a difference in everyone's demeanor before and after the activity.

❑ Secondly, even if you work in a corporate office, I invite you to check out our Self Care for Youth-Serving Professionals Spark Deck. Pull one of the fifty-two cards each day and try to implement the practice on the card. Or shuffle through and select one that jumps out at you. I think you will find that, while you may not be able to have a Perfect Day every day, the micro-practices on the cards will help you on your journey.

NOTES

CHAPTER 18
Do Team Building

Not only are there dozens of books and websites on team building activities, there are also venues that do nothing but team building (ropes courses, escape rooms, etc.), because it is an accepted fact that teams that work well together, perform better.[12]

You may be inclined to think that only a group's manager, principal, or executive director should be the one responsible for thinking about how to build their employees into a team, however, as a Transformational Facilitator, even if you don't wear one of these job titles, this responsibility also falls to you. This is especially salient if the group in front of you will be meeting multiple times (for example, a task force, planning group, or committee). But even if the participants in front of you have never met before, even if they come from a dozen different organizations and will never see each other again, even if you only have them in your session for two hours, helping them feel like a team can improve and increase the benefits they walk away with from your time together.

Because many types of team building activities exist, what follows are some ideas of where to start planning your team building. For actual team building activities within each genre, I direct you to pick up a few books, check out some websites, and look into venues![13]

❏ **Create Shared Purpose**: Fostering connection and a shared sense of responsibility makes it more likely that participants will show up for sub-sequent gatherings. If you are convening a group over multiple sessions, this is crucial. There is nothing worse than a group that gets smaller and smaller as time goes on. Frankly, it is demoralizing for those who remain, and often creates a domino effect. As you plan out the team building portion of your agendas, think about selecting an activity that will generate buy-in and a shared sense of purpose. This can include activities that get at:

> → Why are you here?
> → What motivates you when the going gets tough?
> → What does it mean to pull your weight/be part of a team?

❏ **Build Familiarity**: Knowing and caring about who is in the room can help you accomplish more, faster. Activities that help participants become familiar with each other not only break the ice, they can help people agree more quickly when tough decisions need to be made, or when people are having trouble seeing eye-to-eye. The type of activities to look for in this genre include:

> → Name games
> → Personal and professional history-sharing, and getting-to-know-you activitiess
> → Anything fun

---

[12] See, for example, Google's Project Aristotle findings (Duhigg)

[13] For books, check out (Jones) or (Deming). For venues, search for escape rooms, ropes courses, cooking classes, professional scavenger hunt companies, or volunteering activities.

❑ **Surface Power Dynamics**: These types of activities are especially useful in groups where there are both managers and their supervisees in the room, for example, but also help address power dynamics related to race, gender, and other factors that prevent participants from being fully included. It is tempting to shy away from stirring the pot and letting these issues surface, but that is part of being a Transformational Facilitator; if we are not naming the power dynamics that are inhibiting full inclusion, we cannot ever be fully Transformational. Activities in this genre might address questions such as:

> → In what ways does the leadership of our group reflect our group as a whole? What can we do to create more balance and be more mindful of the effects of our hierarchy?
> → Are our decision-making processes equitable; who gets to decide what, about whom?
> → How are we actively addressing inclusion, race, biases, etc. within this group? In what ways can we improve our practices?

❑ **Identify Skill Contribution**: Understanding everyone's strengths can help during action planning or when working in small groups. Team building activities can be a proactive way of surfacing these skills and looking at how they contribute to collective success. For example:

> → Activities that generate maps, puzzle-pieces, or posters that highlight what skills the group possesses
> → Group-centered personal and professional inventories
> → Activities that assign specific roles and then debrief how that transfers to the current task at hand

❑ **Highlight the Team**: Team Builders, unlike icebreakers, do not have to happen at the start of an engagement; they can happen at any point and even be woven into content that is being covered. Any time you are asking groups to work conscientiously together, you are fostering the development of the team:

> → After any group activity, ask participants to reflect on what skills they brought to accomplishing the goal of the activity
> → Invite participants to express gratitude for others in the group who helped accomplish a goal or task
> → Incorporate team names, language or images into activities and materials

I encourage you, as a Transformational Facilitator, to always be thinking about how the activities and agenda items you are planning foster and support the development of a feeling of "we are a team." And not just amongst participants, but including yourself in that "we" as well. We are all in this work together, and together is better, safer, stronger. This does not mean that we all need to think alike or agree all the time. Rather, it means creating a space where people feel ready to take on challenges together. If you haven't been consistently incorporating team building into your engagements, this is something I'd like to encourage you to try out, and see what a difference it makes! There's a reason it's such a robust industry.

Ways I already do team building.

NOTES

CHAPTER 19
Value Individual Perspectives

In Chapter 22, I will talk about creating community agreements or group norms, and how important this can be for heading off "difficult facilitation situations." One of the reasons that creating agreements/norms can work to prevent trouble down the line is that it helps everyone feel safer and braver. And when we feel safer and braver, we are less likely to default to our fight or flight responses and are better able to learn, grow, and move forward.[14] It has been my experience that conflict is the most generative when we all know what the terms of the engagement are.

Transformational Facilitation aims to elevate participants' voices and put everyone in the room on equal footing. Coming to a shared understanding of the way the group will operate in the room together is essential because it gets everyone on the same page about expectations for conduct. **When we know what is expected of us, we are more easily able to act according to those expectations**. This is a key part of social contract theory,[15] which is underpinned by the idea that we are able to function peaceably in society not because it is natural to us, but because, as a group, we have (consciously or unconsciously) agreed to a set of behaviors. This is what makes community agreements and norms effective, as we are consciously outlining what those behaviors are.

One of the most important shared understandings that a Transformational Facilitator must get across is that there is value in individual perspectives.

Remember, we are doing away with the idea that an "expert" in the room is more important than personal experience. In an "expert" model, the expert is "right," and the rest of us are going to learn what is "right." Once we do away with the expert model, we can place more value on individual opinion and personal perspective sharing. Only when all participants understand and own the value of these perspectives will people be comfortable sharing and contributing in ways that move the conversation forward.

So, how can you, as a Transformational Facilitator, help participants see the value in perspectives? Here are a few thoughts and ideas to get you started:

❑ **Believe it yourself.** Being open to diverse opinions begins with you, as facilitator. Model valuing participant contribution by honestly stating when something is a new idea to you, is different from how you would have thought about it, or when you need clarification.

❑ **State it explicitly**. I do this all the time. Here's how I explain it: "In this workshop we will be using the 'Twitter' model rather than the 'NBC Nightly News' model. This means that instead of one expert sharing their knowledge with everyone, each person in this room will be sharing their own wisdom. You will do much more talking than I do, so get ready!"

---

[14] (Vogel and Schwabe)
[15] (D'Agostino et al.)

❑ **Make it possible**. As you are designing your agenda, keep the idea of personal-experience-sharing central. How can you bring forward the points you want to cover through the voices of participants? Ideas for this are covered throughout this book, especially in Section 4.

❑ **Model it.** When you speak, be mindful of making it clear that you are talking from your personal experience rather than making statements that appear as universally true. So, for example, instead of saying, "Children love candy," try, "I've noticed that most children really seem to get excited when I bring out candy."

❑ **Step back.** As facilitator, it is often tempting to jump in with responses or information, but I encourage you to restrain yourself and wait to see if the answers arise from participants themselves. They almost always will eventually come to the surface if you are patient and set up your questions and activities carefully.

❑ **Allow for divergence**. You do not need everyone in the room to walk away with the same thing. That's right. It is not only acceptable, but preferable that people walk away with what they need. That means that each person will be leaving with something different: A different "aha moment," a different action plan, a different train of thought.

With this in mind, it can be very helpful to state this explicitly (e.g. "We are all here for different reasons, so we will all leave here with different take-aways"), and create your agenda so that a range of viewpoints and learning can surface.

❑ **Jump in**. You will certainly, at one point or another, find yourself in a situation where things are said that are offensive or just plain wrong (the world is NOT flat!). This often results in disagreements or tension arising between participants and, if left unchecked, can take your event off track, especially when it becomes a back-and-forth between two participants while everyone else shifts in their seats and looks at their watches. For this reason, it is imperative that you interrupt.

Jumping in is not easy to do, particularly since you've been working to let these individual perspectives surface. Try to keep in mind that you are interrupting for the benefit of everyone in the room, because there is a difference between "perspective" and "misinformation/bias/slur." The more you practice this skill, the better you will get at it – both at realizing when it is occurring, and stepping in once you've noticed it.

I should also mention here that once you have interrupted the argument or pointed out the error/offense, it is very important to schedule and address the issue at some point with the participant(s). It is not Transformational to say you want people to share their opinions, and then cut them off without following up and explaining why you did so. If there is not time in that moment to mention that you will be following up, then definitely do so during a break or at the earliest opportunity.

❑ **Change your objectives**. As a Transformational Facilitator one of the hardest things to do is to let go of the idea that there is a "right" way of doing things or that your role in the front of the room is to get everyone to do things your way. If you are set on this, you will inevitably stifle new ideas that would otherwise arise from the group. Instead, try to set your expectations differently. For example, instead of the objective, "Everyone will be able to use a tennis racket to hit the ball," try, "Everyone will learn, share, and figure out ways a tennis racket can be used to hit a ball."

You don't have to do all of these at once, but working towards valuing perspectives really starts with you, as facilitator, so go ahead and pick a place to try out how this can work for you.

CHAPTER 20
Adjust the Volume

In my first year as a classroom teacher, I lost my voice. I was completely hoarse for most of the year. It was unclear to me at first why this was the case. I have a strong voice, I love to sing, it made no sense.

Until I realized how loud my classroom was, and how often I was trying to speak over the noise.

This happens more often than you'd think when facilitating adults as well. Particularly because you are asking people to work in pairs or small groups, the noise level in the room often goes way up. In Chapter 15, and again in Chapter 30, I talk about some methods you can use to quiet your group down and make sure everyone can hear each other. In this chapter, I'd like to spend a moment talking about noise, silence, and how we handle talking as a Transformational Facilitator.

❑ **Plan for an ebb and flow**. Just as we think about how long we let participants sit still for, (so that they can comfortably sit when it is time to sit and then jump up ready to move when it is time to move), thinking about the ebb and flow of noise levels in our events can help people talk when it is time to talk, and truly listen when it is time to listen. As you are crafting your agenda, be mindful of the changes in the noise level your activities will cause and plan to vary them accordingly.

❑ **Include an agreement**. As with other behaviors you want to support, adding an agreement (as I discuss in Chapter 22) about side conversations is also very helpful to prevent them from

happening before they start and to serve as a place you can refer back to when they do happen. Participants will often come up with language like, "one voice," "one mic," or even "refrain from side conversations."

❑ **Hold high expectations.** When it is time for individuals to share out with the whole group, make sure that there are no lingering side conversations happening. I honestly think sometimes facilitators let side conversations carry on because they are either afraid of checking an adult on their behavior, or, even more likely because they simply don't notice it - they are so accustomed to it happening. Make sure you are listening and noticing side conversations or other noises. Some suggestions on how to remind people to end side conversations are outlined below.

❑ **Intervene**. If you notice a side conversation happening, you have a few options for intervening, my go-to strategy is to ask the speaker to wait until all of the talking has stopped. There is no reason to tell the side-conversationers to stop talking. Usually when the room falls totally silent, they will stop automatically. Another option is to gently remind the side-conversationers that they need to hold off a moment until the speaker is finished. I know this can sometimes still even make me feel uncomfortable, but when done with a smile, please, and thank you, most people are eager to stop and listen. If you've included an agreement about this, you can simply remind people of the agreement.

❑ **Be consistent about diverting interruptions.** Unless you want to allow people to argue and dialogue across the room, which can spiral out of control quickly and does not allow high-quality airtime to all participants, I recommend putting a stop to interruptions or interjections with a simple, "Let so-and-so finish" and remind participants of your community agreement about interruptions. Then, allow a few minutes to let people turn-and-talk or pair-share about the controversial topic that was causing an argument or dialogue. In this way everyone gets to weigh in, without a giant cross-room argument that can feel unproductive and disruptive. It is also helpful to keep a blank chart paper posted on the wall to serve as a "parking lot," where you can write down and capture those off-topic but potentially useful ideas or concerns for later, freeing you up to move on with the current topic.

❑ **Encourage participants to raise their hands.** While on the one hand this means that you are taking some power back as the facilitator, (in that you get to choose who to call on), on the other hand, you are putting yourself in a position to see the bigger landscape and ensure that everyone has a chance to speak. I find that participants generally automatically do this anyway, so I usually just follow their lead. However, to be safe, you may want to let people know that you would like people to raise their hands if they have something to say.

If many people raise their hands at once, you can call on multiple people at a time, as in, "First Andy, then Cynthia, then Maria," so people know when their turn is coming. You can even write a list of who is next in the speaking order if there is a long line of people waiting to have a turn and you think this will make it easier for you to remember the order.

❑ **Be mindful of how loud of a voice you or participants need to use in order to be heard in the room**. If you or participants need to speak well above a normal talking voice, it's time to reconsider either using a microphone, or eliminating individual sharing altogether, which sometimes simply makes the most sense.

If you are serious about sending the message that individual opinions and voices matter in your events, then keeping an ear out for what you and participants are able to hear is truly important.

Here are a couple of to-dos:

→ If you haven't been already, pause throughout your next engagement to notice the noise levels and see if you're on track.

→ Next time an individual is speaking, look around and notice, are people listening to each other?

→ At your next engagement, keep a count of how many times participants interrupt each other (if at all). If the number is greater than three, try out one of these practices and see if it gets better the next time.

CHAPTER 21
Stay Present and Engaged

During events that use Transformational Facilitation, you, as facilitator, will often find yourself with "down time." Since participants are busy talking with each other, rather than spending the day listening to you, you may find it tempting to sit down and space out, check your phone, or chat with a co-facilitator.

But doing these things can actually suck the energy out of an activity. If you are spacing out or checking your phone, you are sending a message that the activity and conversations, ergo the participants themselves, are not important. Plus, it is when we stop paying attention that other problems begin to arise, problems that may compromise the feeling of safety in the room.

Here are some suggestions for what you can do with yourself while participants are engaged with each other, to remain involved without being overbearing, attuned but not meddling.

❏ **Sit, but listen.** This is probably the least awkward of the options, as you are acting like a fly on the wall. I will often sit down in a corner, nearby participant conversations but not directly at the table, and tune in to what they are talking about. I aim to shift my focus from group to group, so I can catch the gist of what they are covering. I often end up pulling from these snippets I hear during debriefs or later on in the event.

❏ **Walk around.** This can feel slightly more uncomfortable, and even tiring, but if the room is big or participants are confused, sitting in a corner to listen in is not especially helpful. I find that as I walk around people will often stop me to ask questions, questions that they might not otherwise have brought up or had a chance to ask. These are usually clarifying questions about the activity and if I hadn't been walking around and they hadn't had the chance to ask, they may have ended up off-topic or unable to complete the activity! In short, walking around makes you more accessible.

❏ **Find a partner.** When you have an odd number of participants in your group, you have two options, you can either have one pair become a "trio," or you can fill in and be someone's partner. I actually really like doing this. I get a much better sense of the activity when I am a participant, and it also sends the message that I am a learner and engaged on the same level with everyone else. Of course, at first people may be intimidated to be your partner, but in the end I find people welcome my participation.

❏ **Sit with a group.** This is not my favorite option, as I do feel that my presence can influence the way the group interacts, but there are occasions when I will sit down with a group (usually one that has fewer people than other groups), and participate for a while (asking questions like, "What have you come up with?" or "Where are you with the task?"). The other issue with this option is that if another group needs help, they may not feel they can access you. If you do have a group that is off-task or needs deeper clarification of the activity, I recommend sitting down with them for just a few minutes before getting back up and walking around.

Try out one or all of these strategies and see which one(s) feel most natural and useful to you. I think you will find different ones work best for different types of groups or activities, but that, in general, staying engaged and keeping an ear to the ground will keep your event running more smoothly and comfortably.

NOTES

SECTION THREE
TRANSFER POWER TO THE PARTICIPANTS

Those who aspire to be Transformational Leaders are inspired to transfer power over to their employees. But doing this is not as easy as it sounds. Passing over ownership and responsibility, when not done with intention and clear guidance, can leave those to whom these things are being passed feeling overwhelmed, lost, and even resentful.

This is where Transformational Facilitation can be of great service, because empowering participants is one of its core purposes. Each of the tools and strategies outlined in this section is one piece of a great structure designed to build up the confidence and skills of participants so that they are intrinsically motivated to step forward and lead themselves.

At the beginning of the book I shared a quote that I love from Lao Tzu, which really does sum it up: **When the best leader's work is done, the people will say, "We did it ourselves."**[16]

What this means for you as a Transformational Facilitator is that you need to believe and trust each and every participant, student, or employee with all of your heart. A leader, teacher, or facilitator who is transferring power without also transferring trust, is not really transferring power. The *appearance* of power, maybe, but not actual power.

Part of your work as you make your way through this section, therefore, is inner work. It is the process of letting go. It is being willing to do a trust fall, and being confident that participants will catch you. It is abandoning your ego, which may still be

telling you that you, and only you, know what direction everyone should be heading, and handing the map over to the room.

I can tell you from a great deal of personal experience that this is not easy to do.

Before you begin this section, take a minute to reflect on these questions and consider:

In what areas do I already trust participants?

_____

_____

_____

In what areas do I still need to build my trust of participants?

_____

_____

_____

If I let go of controlling outcomes, what am I afraid might happen?

_____

_____

_____

---

[16] Lao Tzu, Tao Te Ching, c. 5-6th century BCE.

NOTES

CHAPTER 22
Create Group Agreements

One of the questions new facilitators often have is what to do in "difficult" facilitation situations. These situations include things like a participant who is:

> → Interrupting other participants
> → Talking for too long, rambling, or getting off-topic when called on
> → Checking his cell phone every few minutes
> → Arguing/combative with other participants
> → Bringing up specific situations/scenarios that seem confidential
> → Being resistant to participating

Obviously, these behaviors do not describe a participant who is fully engaged or on board with the idea of working toward a common goal. Transformational Facilitation puts methods in place that aim to nip these challenges in the bud. For example, the use of pair-share, where one participant shares her partner's ideas out loud instead of her own, and which I cover in Chapter 35, can curb an overly talkative participant. One of my favorite ways to manage all of the possible difficulties, however, is to acknowledge them through creating group agreements — which can also be thought of as norms, values, or whatever term or framework you come up with for your group's "ways of interacting."

In full transparency, lately I've been skipping over this step, particularly when I run workshops where the group is only together for a short period and then will never see each other again. I've also had a number of conversations with facilitators recently about what kinds of norms create the most productive and bravest spaces and feel like I am still learning in this area. I therefore hope that you will add your ideas to my list below, so that we can all get better at this together.

Here are a few ideas to get us all started.

❑ **Create participant ownership of the agreements**. This is done either by having participants generate the agreements themselves, or pick options from a list. One way I've done this is to let them write the idea they invent or select on a sticky note. Once everyone has a note, I have them read the notes out loud, one at time, as they post them up on a piece of chart paper. You can frame this either as ideas everyone will agree to, or simply let each person pick a personal agreement to which they will hold themselves accountable.

❑ **Frame the agreements in positive language**. It is much easier for people to follow a positive directive, than to avoid breaking a rule. Instead of "no side conversations," encourage people to write, "make sure only one person is talking at a time." Instead of "no calling out," reframe it as "raise your hand if you'd like to comment." Explain this to participants before they start writing their agreements if they will be creating them from scratch, and help them reframe their suggestions as needed.

A little side note here: This is also helpful if a participant suggests an agreement that is really negative or inappropriate. For example, when I was a teacher and did this with one of my classes, a student suggested, "No farting," which obviously sent the class into an uproar. Together, we worked to find the root of this suggestion and reframe it positively so that it became, "If you need to use the restroom, raise your hand." There. Much better.

❑ **Agreements can also be aspirational**. These are not a list of rules, and don't have to be just about what teachers refer to as "classroom management," meaning just about participant behavior. They can also be about how participants want to learn and engage. For example, things like "have fun," "think about how this applies to my job," "learn at least one new idea," "step out of my comfort zone," or "meet one new person," can make your list more lively and uplifting.

❑ **Clarify what the agreements mean**. This is important. If someone writes "be respectful," that could mean a lot of different things to a lot of different people. As each participant posts their agreement, check with the group to see if anyone has questions about the meaning of the agreement. If so, ask the participant to explain what they mean.

❑ **Fill in any gaps**. If there is something that you really need as a facilitator that you are worried the group will not come up with or choose, you can contribute to the agreements as well! For me, it is really important that people silence and put away their phones, so I always make a sticky note that says that and then explain what it means when it's my turn to post my note.

❑ **The group does not have to agree to everything on the list.** After everyone has had a chance to contribute an idea, I like to ask the group if there is anything on our list that someone feels they cannot agree to. If there is, then we discuss further what the item means and either make adjustments so that it is agreeable to all, or simply agree to disagree. It is important that everyone is able to call into question any agreements that do not work for them, so keep

at it until you have a list that is workable and understandable to everyone.

❑ **Agree to the role of your agreements.** Are there consequences for breaking agreements? Is this a living document that can be changed when needed? Do they get typed up and signed, like a contract? Do you add to them and revise them every time a new person joins your group? Decisions like these are helpful to think about once you have a list in place.

❑ **Refer to them as needed.** Throughout the engagement, if you find yourself running into an issue, step over to your agreements and point out that we have deviated from one of the items on the list. Honestly, I've only had to do this on a handful of occasions. Generally, once you take the time to create the agreements and have them sitting there up in a prominent place on a wall during the event, people really do tend to remember them.

❑ **Reuse them**. If your group will be meeting more than once, save the agreements either by rolling up the chart paper or by typing them up and handing them out at your next engagement together. If you create agreements with your work colleagues, you can even put them up in each of your meeting rooms, so that they are always there as a reminder. Then, at the start of each meeting, you just need to remind everyone that the agreements are up before starting in on your agenda.

❑ **Skip the agreements, and head straight to needs**. As I mentioned, I've been skipping agreement-creation for the sake of efficiency, but one thing I've been adding in is taking a few minutes to ask participants what they need from me, as the facilitator, to help them fully participate. I really love this framing, as it helps me know how to handle the group, while simultaneously letting the group hear what will be supportive for each person.

❑ **Borrow lists**. As I mentioned in the first bullet point, rather than having participants generate their own ideas, you can give them a list of ideas to choose from. A quick Google search for "List of Meeting Agreements," yields dozens of examples. Hand out copies of your list, and let participants select one or two that they want to either contribute to your group's list, or that they want to hold for themselves.

Creating agreements may seem like a lot of work and even like wasted time, as it usually takes at least 20 minutes, but, especially if you have been finding yourself with difficult facilitation situations cropping up, or if your group is going to meet regularly, it is time really well spent. It is also a great starting point for introducing the idea that from now on, participants are going to be making the "rules" and decisions, rather then having them handed down to them.

There are a lot of creative ways and variations out there for generating the agreements, beyond just using the sticky note method I mention here. If you do an internet search for "community agreements" you will come up with dozens of fun ideas that make it both an engaging and meaningful process.[17]

---

[17] For example, https://www.nsrfharmony.org/wp-content/uploads/2017/10/SettingAgreementsW-Examples_0.pdf or https://engagingschools.org/wp-content/uploads/2014/08/Engaging_Schools_Activators_Group_Agreements_and_Group_Expectations.pdf

NOTES

CHAPTER 23
Create Individual Roles

A hierarchy is already built into your meeting structure. A non-profit board, for example, has a president who runs the meetings, a secretary who takes notes, and a treasurer who gives a financial report. Similarly, in your workplace you may be the manager running the meeting, with an administrative assistant there to take notes and various employees primed to give reports on the status of their projects.

In other situations, there is a more subtle hierarchy. I have often been called in to facilitate meetings of staff and their supervisors. While everyone is ostensibly on equal footing while I am in the room running the show, in reality, there is still an underlying deference to the supervisor, especially, as often happens, if that supervisor is unable to sit back and let themselves be "just another participant."

Of course, the group in front of you will always be heterogeneous, because even when everyone has the same job title or role, people may have varying levels of prior knowledge of the subject, have more experience with the organization, or simply arrive with different degrees of excitement. In addition, race, gender, language ability, etc. all contribute to a hierarchy that often remains unstated, but that still plays out in how fully and comfortably participants are able to engage.

Here are a few thoughts on ways to use role assignment to help balance the playing field and ensure everyone feels empowered to step forward.

❑ **Let them decide.** In small group projects, you can let each group pick who will do each role based on who is more excited to take notes, say, and who has a watch and can keep track of time. Use this process when you feel confident that

the small groups can equitably work their roles out. It is actually a great practice for a group to self-assign their roles and consider their strengths or what they feel they can challenge themselves to work on.

Some examples of roles that participants might like to create or take on could include (I have left space for you to add your own ideas):

→ Timekeeper
→ Notetaker
→ Spokesperson
→ Artist/graphic recorder
→ Facilitator/process leader
→ Coach
→ Dynamics observer
→ Feedback provider
→
→
→
→

❑ **Intentionally assign roles.** This works best when you know the group and want to raise up or encourage certain participants to build a skill. For example, if you work with someone who would benefit from a specific role but may not have the courage to ask for it, assign the role to them and explain why.

❑ **Randomly assign roles.** If self-selecting roles seems like it might be difficult for a pair or small group, roles can be randomly assigned by having each person count off and then announcing, "Ones will be the note-takers, twos will be the facilitators," etc. This is probably the fastest way to get people into their roles, if your time is tight.

- ❏ **Collectively decide on the roles you will need.** Sometimes the needs are obvious: someone to take notes, someone to chart responses on the whiteboard, someone to keep track of time or make sure that the groups stays on task. But in many situations, you can work with the group to decide what roles will be needed. This is particularly true if you are planning an event. A fun way to come up with the roles you will need is to do the sorting activity I cover in Chapter 39, but any brainstorming activity will work.

- ❏ **Make sure the roles are clear.** It is impossible for anyone to do their role well if they don't know exactly what they are supposed to be doing. Even for something that seems straight-forward, like notetaking, spending a minute quickly clarifying exactly what that person needs to do helps people fill their role with confidence.

- ❏ **Switch roles often.** Part of your job as a Trans-formational Facilitator is to encourage and excite new and innovative ways of thinking. When we always play the same part, we tend to develop a bit of mono-vision, always looking at things from the same perspective. For example, if the same person is always giving the financial report, they may tune out when an agenda item on the table does not have any financial implications. Encourage active participation and fresh thinking by creating opportunities for participants to switch roles.

A quick personal example here: As the leader of my band, I was always deciding which songs we would rehearse each week, and then providing feedback to the musicians after each song we played. This was not only exhausting to me, but also disincentivized my bandmates from listening to each other or thinking about how the songs could be done better. I decided to switch things up, so each week a different bandmate became the leader for that week, calling the songs and opening up a discussion on feedback after each tune. The change in energy was palpable, and I found much more enjoy-ment and relaxation in the rehearsals.

- ❏ **Offer support and encouragement.** Particularly when people have grown accustomed to passively participating, suddenly being asked to take a role within a class, meeting, workshop, or event can feel like a lot of pressure to some participants. Make sure you offer praise and encouragement to people as they fulfill their roles, and be there for them when they have questions or run into a stumbling block.

- ❏ **Let people play their role.** There is nothing worse than assigning a role, and then not giving people the autonomy to actually do their job. If you are asking someone to lead something, let them lead it. It may not go 100% the way you wanted it to the first time, but with practice, you will find that people quickly improve. This is a chance for you to let go. Take it.

Empowering participants through picking and assigning roles may seem like a heavy lift, but I encourage you to try it and notice how the energy perks up. On the following page I offer a Think Sheet that covers a very specific example of a role-assigned activity. Before you read it, take a minute to reflect on the following questions:

What typical roles do participants in my current engagements play?

_____

_____

_____

What roles could I envision participants playing?

_____

_____

_____

What are my worries surrounding roles?

_____

_____

_____

Peer Coaching "Think Sheet"

Increasingly in my workshops, I have been setting up peer-coaching opportunities, which enable participants to provide coaching to each other in areas they are struggling in. In reviewing the feedback from a recent session, it was many of my participants' favorite activity, so let me share a few ideas with you here.

First of all, peer coaching capitalizes on the idea of giving each participant a specific role. This means it helps ensure everyone is fully and actively engaged. If you have been noticing a lack of engagement in your workshops or meetings, this might be a great tool to try.

Secondly, peer coaching lands squarely in the sphere of Transformational Facilitation because the activity runs itself and each participant becomes an expert and leader. Honestly, during peer-coaching time, when it is properly set up and thought out, I often sit quietly and listen while keeping my eye on my timer; that's it.

Thirdly, once everyone gets the idea and knows how it works, peer-coaching can be done in just a couple of minutes in any meeting or class. In fact, it makes a fantastic standing agenda item.

Here's how I run the sessions:

1. Prior to the engagement, I prepare a handout with open-ended questions to help participants think through the issue they will be bringing to their coach. Questions I generally include on the handout include:

> → What is the issue?
> → When is it happening?
> → What is happening to you when the issue is taking place?
> → What is happening for others?" etc.

You will see below how I use the list, but the general idea is to allow people a chance to reflect on their selected issue using these questions before they actually meet with their coach, and to provide the coach with some open-ended questions to get the process started, (although I find that many people do not need the paper and are easily able to ask appropriate open-ended questions).

2. As I introduce the coaching, I reminded people to turn off their "right reflex," which is a term a colleague recently introduced me to. When our right reflex is engaged, our tendency is to quickly generate solutions to a problem, rather than continue to listen openly. I introduce the concept to people and encourage them to refrain from asking questions like, "Have you tried X?", which is really a solution disguised as a question.

3. Next, I ask people to count off to form groups of three. This mixes up the tables where people are sitting and puts them into new groups for a fresh perspective. I encourage each group to move their chairs and find a comfortable spot to work together.

4. Once everyone is settled, I ask them to decide on an A, B, and C person in their group. For the purposes of our coaching, we start the first round with A presenting their issue as the "coached person"; B serving as the person asking questions (I do not use the word "coach" because I want to reinforce that their role is to ask questions); and C playing the role of observer, who will be tasked with providing feedback to the coach at the end of the session. C provides feedback on whether they were able to keep asking open-ended questions or if their "right reflex" kicked in.

5. I set a timer for five to ten minutes, depending on how much time I have allotted for the activity, and let them start. When time is up, the observer has two minutes to provide feedback. During this time, the coached person (A) is also able to give feedback to the coach (B) if they want to.

6. After we are done, the participants switch roles. B becomes the person being coached, C becomes the question-asker, and A becomes the observer. At the end of this round we switch one more time, so that everyone has a chance to try out each role.

At first people might feel that five to ten minutes is too long, and they run out of things to say, but by the third round, they usually figure out how to fill the time and get deeper into the issues they are addressing.

As one participant recently noted, "I loved being able to speak about issues with others."

If you decide to run this activity, here are few things to consider:

❑ **Let them choose**. I keep the prompt fairly open but still on-topic for the workshop. For example, in a recent workshop on Positive Behavior Guidance it was simply, "What is a behavior in youth that you are seeing in your program that you would like to address?"

❑ **Give them more time.** After the first round, one group of participants recently told me they wanted more time for the observer to give feedback, so I extended my original time from one minute to two minutes. Luckily, we had the extra minutes to spare because I really wanted to honor their depth of consideration and conversation.

❑ **Keep an ear out.** During the five minutes, the person being coached should be doing most of the talking, with the question-asker only minimally involved. The observer should not say anything, and all solutions should be coming from the person being coached. If you notice groups falling into other practices, redirect them so that everyone has a turn to really be heard out and clearly think about good questions to ask.

After the three rounds, I ask everyone to return to their original tables and talk about how it was for them to participate in the peer coaching. I also ask them how they could envision bringing what they learned back to their staff or students. In another recent set of evaluations, several people commented that they wanted to try the peer coaching with the people they work with.

And one more reason to start using peer-coaching? It means you no longer have to come up with all of the solutions. Now, instead of asking you (or a supervisor) for help, participants will be more comfortable either coming up with solutions on their own, or turning to a peer or colleague for support.

CHAPTER 24
Elevate Participant Responses

As a Transformational Facilitator, I like to imagine myself as almost invisible within a meeting or workshop. Or at least semi-transparent. This means that as much as possible, I aim to let the noise and ideas arise from participants, not from me. This seems like it wouldn't be so hard, but facilitators have millions of little ways of inadvertently taking center stage.

☐ **You are not a microphone.** One prime example of how facilitators accidentally take the mic is their tendency to reiterate responses shared by participants. The intentions are good, I am quite sure they are doing so to amplify and add weight to the comment or contribution. However, echoing participant responses sets up a dynamic in which participants become conditioned to listen to you, as facilitator, rather than to each other. And that's the opposite of what a Transformational Facilitator wants to do.

Next time you are tempted to repeat back a comment from a participant, catch yourself and simply let the comment sit where it is. If others in the room could not hear the contribution, invite the participant to repeat what they said, rather than doing the repeating for them. How does that feel?

☐ **Let the comment stand.** It is also helpful to be mindful of not always dialoging with, commenting on, or adding to participant contributions. If the contribution raises a response in your mind, remember that it is probably doing so in everyone else's mind as well. Why do YOU always get to be the one to add to or amplify what a participant says? Again, let the comment sit and move on, or let others in the space be the ones to respond as you keep your thoughts to yourself.

The one exception to this is when someone says something that is hurtful or undermines someone else in the group. In this situation it is imperative that you step in to ensure that everyone continues to feel safe and willing to contribute.

☐ **Chart responses.** If your intention is to validate and elevate participant contributions, write their responses up on a whiteboard or piece of chart paper. Bullet points work well for this, and noting just the key words or using abbreviations works well. Better yet, so that you can fully focus on the participants, ask for a volunteer to chart for you. Once the idea is charted, check back in with the contributor to make sure you captured their thought accurately. "Did I get this right?" If a volunteer is charting, let that person check back with the participant. Look at how you are sharing the stage! Now move on and chart the next response.

In this strategy you are validating contributions without placing yourself in the central role of being microphone. You are a catcher of ideas, rather than the voice of those ideas. It may seem like a subtle difference, but in the quest to empower and raise participant voices, it is an extremely vital shift.

❑ **Refer to their responses.** Nothing says, "I am listening," better then returning to a participant comment later in the meeting, workshop, or class. "As ___ pointed out…" "Building off of what ____ said…" "This goes back to what ____ suggested…" are all ways of elevating the ideas that have been raised by participants. You can also encourage participants to follow your lead and refer back to comments other participants have made when adding in comments of their own.

I know that old habits are hard to break, and that things like refraining from repeating participant comments can be so automatic we don't even realize we are doing it. If this is something you'd like to work on, practice by really listening to the comments, and then taking a deep breath after each one (perhaps as you chart it!), so you are creating space for it, rather than filling that silence with your own voice. I am quite confident that after a few tries, this, too, will feel like second nature.

NOTES

CHAPTER 25
Stay Curious

We come together as a group for many reasons. You may be hosting a book club with friends, running a meeting at work, holding a family discussion, or teaching an art class for senior citizens. Whatever you are leading, an opportunity often arises to solicit input (e.g. "What book should we read next?"). Here's something I know to be true about myself: As soon as the brainstorming starts, I find myself automatically evaluating each idea as it arises ("Oooooh, I love that one!" or "Oh, no way, that will never work"). This is something I have to continuously be mindful of, because when we turn on our evaluation brains, we are, by definition, narrowing down the possibility of embracing truly innovative thoughts. And that is not what a Transformational Facilitator wants to do at all.

There are many books and resources available that can help you choose and run excellent brainstorming activities,[18] so instead, what I offer here are some things to think about as you go about finding and executing those activities.

❑ **Name the problem.** Prepare yourself and your participants by naming the problem. As in, "We're going to brainstorm a bunch of ideas. My challenge to us all is to not judge the ideas as they arise, but, instead, answer questions about each idea. Let's stay curious! This is, obviously, easier said than done, so we will be using a fun process to help everyone stay in 'open mind' mode a little longer."

❑ **Brainstorm questions, instead of ideas.** Start by asking everyone to brainstorm just one key idea. Using our book club example, each person would be asked to write a suggestion for the next book on an index card, anonymously. As facilitator, collect the cards and read off the first one. Now allow participants a few minutes to write down a question they have about that choice on a new index card, encouraging everyone to come up with the most creative and open-ended questions they can think of. ("Why do you think that would be a good choice for our group?" "What interesting things have you heard about the book or author?"). By brainstorming questions, you are intentionally encouraging people to open up their thinking.

❑ **Let people answer the brainstormed questions in as many ways as possible.** If you have participants generate questions, you can also have them answer those questions, as creatively as possible. ("I think it would be a good choice for our group because none of us have ever read anything by that author before.") Anyone can answer the questions, regardless of who generated the original idea.

❑ **Allow time for objective commenting and information gathering.** Invite participants to turn to a partner to discuss anything they know about each brainstormed idea. ("I've read that the author wrote this book while on her honeymoon and that it is actually part autobiographical." "I know that the author published this book, his first, when he was eighty-five years old.").

---

[18] Check out (Scannell and Mulvilhill) or (Miller).

Remind everyone to refrain from making judgements about the idea, and to keep their discussions focused on building up more information about it instead.

❑ **Ask your own set of questions.** Come prepared with a set of questions that will be used with each idea. Keep the questions open-ended with an eye toward generating a deeper understanding of the idea. Some questions you could pose for each idea might include:

> → What do you like about this idea?
> → What do you think would be difficult about this idea?
> → What additional ideas does this idea make you think of?

The practice of remaining open-minded and focusing on questioning during the idea-generation process allows participants to feel that even if their suggestion is not, ultimately, acted upon, they still had airtime and thought dedicated to their offering. And having a chance to think about each idea may (and will!) generate new ideas that participants hadn't even been thinking of originally, ("Oh, right, I loved that first book she wrote and feel that it is less heavy than the one that was just suggested, we should consider that one for our club instead!")

I am aware that the book club example may be too far off topic for many of you reading this chapter to fully bite into, so I challenge you to think of a scenario in your daily interactions where this strategy might work for you. Here are a few more to help get your own ideas going:

→ In a work setting, after asking staff to brainstorm ideas to improve "X" about your organization (let's say, staff retention), participants may generate ideas like "higher salaries," "more vacation time," "better working conditions," etc. Questions they could discuss after each idea is offered might include, "How do you see this idea contributing to higher employee retention?" "Have you ever seen this used as an effective strategy? How did it play out?" or "Would this encourage YOU to stay in your job? Why or why not?"

→ At home, as a parent, you may ask your children for ideas about something, like what they'd like to do on a day off of school. Ideas may include the amusement park, a movie, or just hang out at home with their friends. Questions that you could ask about each idea are, "What would be fun about that activity?" "Have you done something similar before? What did you like about it?" or "Would this be fun for all of us? Why do you think that?"

→ On a fundraising committee you're part of, ask questions about the various ideas that come up while discussing themes for your annual gala, such as "Sixties Rock and Roll," "Lending a Hand," or "Pizza with a Purpose". Questions could be "What about this theme would be fun for donors?" "How does this theme relate to our mission?" "What kinds of additional fundraising activities could we do leading up to the gala related to the theme to increase revenue?"

→ In a class, you may find yourself (as I once did!) asking students for ideas on what they think the most popular work of art ever created is. "The Mona Lisa," "David," "The Scream." And the questions to discuss could be, "Why do you think that is the most popular work of art?" "What about the piece do you think people like/what do you like about it?" "Are there any other artworks that you know of by the same artist that are as well known? If so, what is similar or different about the pieces?"

The basic concept here is that instead of evaluating an idea (making judgements), you are encouraging everyone, yourself included, to answer questions and **stay curious**. By asking questions you are helping to scaffold the curiosity process, especially when you all are new at keeping your minds open.

Ultimately, by keeping an open mind and not jumping to shut down ideas, you are creating the conditions for empowerment - because all ideas are considered and weighed before any decisions are made. With time and practice, I think you will find that you are better able to stretch your own ability to stay open as well.

CHAPTER 26
Wait

It may seem obvious, but thinking takes time. Why then, when we are running meetings or workshops, do we rush the process and call on the first hand that gets raised? If you truly want to have an equitable distribution of voices in your engagements, and keep people motivated, focused, and empowered during the event, it is important to allow time for participants to formulate their thoughts before you ask people to share out. If not, you are only going to hear from people who think quickly on their feet, or feel comfortable raising a hand and talking in front of a group, while the rest sit back and recede into their seats.

In fact, not allowing adequate think time, and, likewise, not having a system for people to share equitably, is one of the key factors as to why, for example, girls fall behind in math in school[19] (they are drowned out by their male classmates who often shout out answers out of turn, are overlooked by teachers as they sit with quiet hands raised, etc.). Similarly, people from different cultural backgrounds may have various norms around speaking order, disclosure of ideas, etc.,[20] that make allowing adequate think time imperative to ensure everyone has had a chance to work through their thoughts.

Giving adequate think time and being creative about how you ask participants to share actually benefits everyone; since you know the first thought that pops into your head isn't always the best one. So here are a few tips to help you make it happen:

❑ **Count to five.** After you pose a question to the group, resist the temptation to call on the first hands that go up. Instead, count to five and wait to see if more hands get raised. Those five seconds of silent wait time may feel like an eternity, but you will be surprised by how just those few moments help so many more people gather their thoughts.

❑ **Keep track.** Be mindful of calling on the same person over and over again. It is tempting to do, because you want to keep things moving and there are always a handful of people who are super eager to contribute. If you need to, keep a list of participants and make a little mark each time you call on someone, making sure that by the end of the engagement, you've called on everyone.

❑ **Use pair-shares.** I talk about using the strategy in many different scenarios, but it works extremely well for making sure you are allowing both think time and equity of voice. After you pose a question to the group, allow partners to discuss their responses with each other, and then - and this is essential - *have them share out the response their partner just told them*, rather than repeating their own response. People often feel more comfortable sharing someone else's ideas, so for those who are reluctant to share their own thoughts, this works really, really well.

---

[19] (American Association of University Women)
[20] (Reaven)

Someone recently asked me what I do when someone misrepresents their partner's ideas, which does occasionally happen. The best route here is to check with the partner after their idea has been shared, to make sure it was done accurately. If they say, "no," then give them a chance to express themselves directly.

❑ **Eliminate asking whole-group questions.** By this I mean asking one question of the whole group and then letting everyone (or even a handful of people) share their responses to the whole group. Eliminating this habit may seem impossible, but, especially in large groups, I really only like to use whole-group share out as a way of hearing what conclusions or ideas small groups or pairs came up with. What's the point of asking a large group a question, if only a few people get to respond, or everyone gets to respond and it takes 30 minutes? During this time everyone is either simmering with their own thoughts or shut down because a response has already been given and you're simply promoting a conversation between yourself and one or two or three other people. That is not Transformative! Challenge yourself to reduce or completely do away with whole-group questions and notice how it shifts the focus of your engagements.

We often use questions to the large group as a quick and easy way to interject some interaction into our event. In reality, the strategy ends up only being interactive for the people being called on to respond, and is not true engagement. If you find yourself tempted to use this strategy often, I encourage you to look for more authentic interaction activities, like a the Gallery Walk I cover in Chapter 41, the brainstorming ideas I mention in

Chapter 25, or Peer Coaching, which you can read about in Chapter 23.

Remember, in Transformational Facilitation *the purpose is to get everyone to participate equally* and to their fullest ability. That cannot happen if only some voices get heard.

Take a minute to reflect on this:

When have you felt that your voice was truly heard? What were the conditions?

_____

_____

_____

When have you felt that your voice was not heard? What were the conditions? What could have been done differently?

_____

_____

_____

What is one way you currently help everyone be heard?

_____

_____

_____

CHAPTER 27
Ask What People Want to Learn

One of the tools that teachers learn about and are often asked to use in their lessons is called a "KWL" chart. It is a method that was introduced by Donna Ogle,[21] which is easy to use and has a lot of research showing its effectiveness. Here's what it looks like:

[Chart]
K = Know
W = Want to Know
L = Learned

I have used this with adults in workshops or as part of a meeting when I am introducing a new concept or we are about to discuss a problem. I find it very useful for helping participants anchor and connect what we are learning and discovering in their own knowledge and desire to know.

Here's how it works in a meeting setting:

1. Open by introducing the topic, as in, "Our next agenda item is on our new timesheet system." Make sure everyone understands what the topic is!

2. Invite participants to share what they already *know* about "timesheets" in your organization, and chart their responses under the "K" column, on the left hand side. If you think people might struggle to come up with responses, have them brainstorm with a partner first. In this example, some responses under the "Know" column I might expect to see are:

> → Timesheets are due the last Friday of each month
> → Timesheets are currently a document on our employee portal
> → You need to download, attach, and email the sheet after you complete it
> → Timesheets take about 10 minutes to fill in

3. After all of the responses are charted, it's time to ask participants what they Want to Know about the new timesheets. By asking what their questions are, you are both helping them formulate what information they will be looking for, while also cluing you in to what details and information you should aim to cover. Once again, you can ask participants to simply share out to the whole group, or first discuss with a partner in order to collect their thoughts before sharing. Some responses I might expect in this center column might be:

> → When will timesheets be due in the new system?
> → Will they take a long time to fill out?
> → How do we access and submit the timesheets?
> → What is different about the new timesheets?

4. Now that you've gotten all of the questions out on the table, it's time to learn! Even with something as dry as a new timesheet system, there are many ways to use Transformational

---

[21] (Ogle)

Facilitation to make the topic interactive and aid learning. For some ideas, check out the "jigsaw activity" I outline in Chapter 42 or, for this particular example, the Venn diagram I discuss in Chapter 40.

5. At the end of this agenda topic, once all of the information has been learned and shared, it is time to complete the "L" column. Once again, you can have participants turn-and-talk to share what they are taking away before sharing out with the larger group. Record their responses in the last column. In our example, I would expect to see:

> → The new timesheets are located on a new server under folder X.
> → The IT department will be sending out passwords next week.
> → Our badges will automatically log our time, so we need to remember to scan them, otherwise we will have to go back in and edit.
> → Timesheets will update in real time, no need to "submit" them.

6. At this point I would suggest doing a closing activity that captures any questions participants still have, as I cover in Chapters 45 or 50.

Will this take more time? Well, yes, it may take more time in the moment, so you need to plan your agenda accordingly, but I am willing to bet you money that you will have less questions from staff later, which will save you time in the long run.

Using a KWL is a fun way to dive into a topic while simultaneously acknowledging what participants are already bringing into the room around the topic. Plus, research demonstrates that the technique is effective in helping people learn![22]

---

[22] (Shelly et al.)

Desire to Know "Think Sheet"

Last year, as the New Year rolled around, I started thinking about how I facilitate future-action in the workshops I run, (meaning, how I get people to actually take action after they leave my engagements), and how this can be translated into new year's resolutions and the strategy of helping people identify what they want to learn.

As a Transformational Facilitator, I always make sure everyone leaves my workshops with a clear plan in hand. These are usually a series of small actions that they commit to take in the next day, week, or month that they have slowly accumulated over the course of the workshop, and that they commit to in writing before they leave, as I outline in Section 5 of this book. Because I promote and ascribe to the Spark Method, these action items are small, easy to achieve, and tied to their personal goals. Additionally, people generally feel optimistic and confident that they can follow through after they've been catapulted out of the relative calm of the workshop space and back into their hectic "real" lives.

In many ways, this is not dissimilar to typical New Year's resolutions. We close out our year thinking about a laundry list of things we'd like to accomplish in the coming twelve months, invigorated by the prospect of starting over again and sticking to our plans. Our lists may contain concrete achievements, like running a 5K, volunteering at a shelter once a month, calling a good friend every weekend. Or they may be more focused on habit shifts or personal improvement, such as attempting to focus on the positive, listing gratitudes, or yelling less at our kids (ahem). We often even build up action steps around our plans, to help us stay on track

(there are more and more apps for this!), or join forces with a friend or relative to form accountability partnerships. Many or our items eventually fade away (er, that 5K), bowled over by circumstance and life, but many actually come to fruition and help us feel motivated to start a new list as the next year rolls around.

As I started thinking about our New Year's resolutions and their relationship to my work in Transformational Facilitation, however, I realized that we have other ways at our disposal. What if instead of focusing on concrete lists of what we plan to achieve by the end of the year or upon leaving the workshop, we open our year and our workshops with a question, not about what we will do or accomplish - but what we will be left with when we are done. The question shifts from being centered on, "What will you do this year/after you leave this workshop?" to focusing on, "**What do you hope to get out of this year/session?**"

My New Year's resolution list shifts dramatically with this small change in the question, most importantly because it assumes I have a level of personal knowledge about what is currently missing. For example, instead of trying to call my friends every Sunday, what I'm really hoping to get out of the year is more and deeper connections with friends. I'm not as interested in yelling less at my kids as I am in creating more peace and tranquility at home. And that 5K, what I'm really hoping for is to achieve some measurable level of physical activity. This change in question gets below the surface, to the heart of what I really want out of the year, or workshop.

So here is an action item for you this New Year (or next time you attend a personal or professional development event): As you create your lists of New Year's hopes and goals, try asking yourself, "What do I hope to get out of this year?" (instead of generating a list of activities or goals), and see how it shifts your list. Likewise, as you step into your first days of facilitation in the new year, try asking your participants not only what they plan to *do* when they leave your space, but open your session with a question: "What do you hope to walk away with from our time together?" Note these responses down, use them as a roadmap as you are generate action steps, and encourage everyone to hold on to this underlying motivation as they leave your event and enter back into their world.

NOTES

CHAPTER 28
Believe in the Knowledge in the Room

Transformational Facilitation continually strives to raise everyone in the room through all of the many practices the facilitator intentionally brings in. From setting up conversations so that everyone has airtime, to running activities that encourage shared decision-making power, to supporting divergent opinions, no one single strategy creates this environment. Rather, it is through the use of multiple strategies and approaches that everyone is lifted up.

It is also through the belief, on the part of the facilitator, that the group has the power and tools they need to be their own guides and leaders. This is that feeling of "trust" I keep referring to. This is essential for many reasons, but especially for empowering participants.

When running workshops or teaching a class, this can be especially tricky. Ostensibly, a facilitator, teacher, lecturer, or professor is brought in to share their expertise. For example, I recently was asked to run a workshop on how to include fun and engaging literacy activities in afterschool programs. You're probably guessing that I have some super-knowledge about this topic that I was bringing to the group; a veritable sage ready to dispense my superior skills to a room full of novices. But that isn't at all true.

Some small steps you can take to help you shift your mindset and turn up the learning and engagement for participants include the following actions.

❑ **Bring out the knowledge that is already in the room.** Because, trust me, it is there. Rather than spending our time together showing a million ways to include literacy activities (which anyone with access to Pinterest could do equally well), in the workshop I reference above, I offered a few examples, and then asked participants to share with each other all of the ways they are already doing it. In this way, I set participants up to be the teachers, giving them space to revisit what they already knew and allowing them to build on each other's ideas.

❑ **Let them answer the questions.** If a participant raises a question at any point during the workshop, rather than answering myself, I turn the question back to the group. The responses they offer are always better than anything I would have thought of on my own, and the spirit of helping each other sets everyone up as both an expert and a learner. As with all Transformational Facilitation techniques, the hierarchy is erased and we are all on equal footing in our quest to learn something new and useful.

❑ **Create your agenda carefully.** Operate on the assumption that the knowledge is already in the room and that your sole job is to help people find that wisdom within themselves and each other. That's it. Create the conditions. As you think about your agenda, focus on the methods you will use to get to the content as intentionally as you do on the content itself. You will be amazed at how much people learn and how much they're able to act on what they've learned.

If you're not sure where to start, check out my ideas for eliminating lectures in Chapter 29, the gallery walk activity I outline in Chapter 41, or revisit the peer coaching model I talk about in Chapter 23. Be mindful of how much space you are occupying in the agenda, and replace "your time" with time for participants to discuss, learn, and create with each other.

Facilitating an engagement where everyone's voices is heard is hard, but if we are serious about the ideals of equity and empowerment, it needs to be done anyway. I realize that this particular chapter may make many of you uncomfortable. After all, you have probably spent many years developing the skills and knowledge that brought you in front of your group in the first place. I hear you. It *is* hard. Do it anyway.

Here are a few reflection questions to help you think through how you can put this into action:

In what ways do I already access and honor the knowledge that participants show up with?

In what ways do I tend to overlook their knowledge?

What steps can I take to raise up the knowledge and wisdom that participants already possess?

CHAPTER 29
Reduce (or Eliminate) Lectures

A central tenet of Transformational Facilitation is to limit (or eliminate!) lectures. And by lectures, I mean all sorts of "people talking at the front of the room for long periods of time," from keynotes to panels to experts. Let's take a moment here to break these down a bit and notice exactly why they stray from the main point of being a Transformational facilitator and what you could substitute instead.

Keynotes: According to Merriam-Webster, a keynote is "the fundamental or central fact, idea, or mood; the first and harmonically fundamental tone of a scale." Let that sink in for a minute. The keynote is supposed to set the tone for the event. If you have a central figure giving a 20-minute talk, no matter how inspiring that lecture is, it is still one person talking at everyone else for 20 minutes. Is that the tone you want to set for your event?

I didn't think so.

Here are some alternative ideas for a keynote at your next event:

❑ **Do a giant full-room pair-share** (covered in Chapter 35) where everyone discusses the key themes of the event with various partners. For example, if it is a conference about climate change, some questions you could have participants discuss might be: What do you do in your personal life to address climate change? What do you do in your work life to address climate change? What do you think the most important step the world needs to take to address climate change should be and why? Etc.

❑ **Run an icebreaker** (covered in Chapter 17)! I know it might sound impossible, but depending on layout (e.g. are you seating people in rows or at tables?), even with 200 people you can get people up and moving and having fun.

❑ **Turn participants into the keynote speakers** by asking everyone to write down a sentence on an index card about either why they are excited to be at the event, what they hope to get out of being at the event, or something important/inspiring they know about the topic. Invite participants to come up and read their cards at the mic, or collect the cards and have a reader share them out.

Panels: I love the concept; gather up a bunch of rockstar practitioners and let them pass the mic for a short period of time. Sometimes there's even time for participants to ask questions and have the panelists directly respond, which seems almost interactive.

But mostly panels are just a series of lectures, and, unfortunately, panelists' lectures often seem to be less prepared and inspiring than keynote speakers' contributions. Of course, as with a keynote speaker, we may be inspired for a moment, quickly jotting down a key phrase or something we want to make sure we remember, but mostly we are passively sitting and listening, and this is not transformational. During panels I often find myself cringing, thinking about how many of the dozens or hundreds of people in attendance have as much wisdom as the people up on the chairs, but they aren't being given a mic.

Here are some alternative ideas for panels at your next event:

❑ **Create small group mini-panels of participants.** This works really well if your participants are already grouped at tables of eight to ten people. Prepare your panelist questions, and then, going around the table, have each participant respond for two minutes. Everyone has the right to pass if they don't want a turn being the panelist, but I think you'll notice that most people take their turn. If you have enough time, after they've had their two minutes, they can take and respond to a question or two from their table before the next "panelist" responds. It is a good idea to change the question up every two to three people, so the responses don't become redundant, or give participants a list of four to five questions they can choose to respond to.

❑ **Host a World Cafe.** In this method, participants move tables (or even go into breakout rooms if you have enough space), and discuss a key question at each rotation. You can find detailed directions and even hire a professional "host" through theworldcafe.com if you want to bring someone in to run the cafe process for you. It is a great way to turn participants into panelists to explore a topic.

❑ **Have table groups collectively create posters about a topic or question.** Choose one of the questions you would have otherwise asked a panelist, and then have each group (or a handful if you have a very large number of participants) share their posters. Hang them up around the room and soak in all of those ideas and knowledge.

❑ **Hold Open Space.** I recently attended an "unconference" that used the principles of Open Space, which is a gathering format developed in the 1980s by Harrison Owen. I have, myself, found that some of the most useful interactions I experience at conferences and meetings are during the breaks and unscheduled times. Open Space leans into this truth by allowing participants to self-organize and hold the conversations that they want to hold. To learn more about how Open Space works, visit www.openspaceworld.org.

Expert Talks: By this I mean a Ted Talk-type of lecture that I often see in workshops or at conferences. The problem isn't that the person is an expert; certainly, we all have something to learn from people who know more about a topic than we do. The issue lies in the WAY that these expert-presentations take place: In most cases, the format is a lecture, occasionally with time for participant questions thrown in, that is often accompanied by PowerPoint (which I already covered in Chapter 6).

While I do encourage you to seek out experts and their research, this is where Transformational Facilitation really kicks in. Can you integrate "expert" level information into your workshop, conference, or meeting without having a single person up in the front of the room talking at participants? Yes! Of course you can. But the "expert" needs to brought along for the ride (perhaps you are the "expert" I am referring to!).

Here are some ideas for including an expert, without the lecture:

❑ **Set up an "ask-an-expert" activity.** Encourage participants to prepare questions for the expert on index cards. Allow only three minutes for the expert to respond. After each question and response, give participants three minutes to discuss their thoughts on what the expert shared with a partner or in a small group (e.g. What is something that you heard that you were already familiar with? What is something that was new information for you? Did you agree/disagree with anything? How could you apply this in your work? etc.). The discussion may generate new questions, so you might want to collect additional index cards after each round.

❑ **Invite participants to be the experts instead of bringing in outside speakers.** I have often worked with constituents to help them facilitate content at an event with their peers. I recommend doing a "call for facilitators" with a note that you will support anyone who would like to share (sometimes a personal invitation helps!). Then...

❑ **Introduce your expert to Transformational Facilitation**(!). If you're going with an outside expert, choose people who you know will be interactive and transformative in their approach. These are the people who won't stand up and lecture, but will work to make their content accessible, engaging, interactive, etc.

Lectures and talks are tempting because, frankly, they are relatively easy. All you need is someone willing to get up in front of the room and speak. But I strongly encourage you to think about the message this sends to participants about who matters and reconsider how to use participants' time next time you are gathering for an engagement - so that everyone has a chance to speak and be heard.

NOTES

CHAPTER 30
Use a Talking Piece

Sending visual or auditory cues to participants helps them know what is going on and what to expect. One cue I have found helpful is to use a "talking piece" during whole-group sharing times. Put simply, a talking piece is an object that participants hold when it is their turn to speak. The visual cue that the object brings shows the rest of the participants that it is their turn to be quiet and listen.

The use of a talking piece falls under the category of empowering participants because, when used equitably (meaning, when it gets passed with equal amounts of time over the course of the engagement to every participant), it gives everyone a chance to have the floor.

Here are a couple of ideas for bringing a talking piece into your facilitation practice:

❑ **Let participants create the piece.** I do this by providing each participant with a 1.5in x 8.5in strip of colored paper. Invite participants to write one "rule of thumb" for being a good listener onto their strip of paper. Have participants introduce themselves and their rule to a partner, then go around the room and have pairs introduce their partner and the rule that person came up with. As each rule is shared, tape it to a paper-towel tube. By the time everyone has had a turn to share, you have a colorful object, full of everyone's ideas, that you can use for the rest of the engagement.

❑ **Use a rain stick.** Rain sticks are fun because the beautiful, calming sound they make can serve double-duty as your attention-getting signal. Turn the stick until the group is quiet, then pass it to whomever's turn it is to speak.

❑ **Use a microphone.** Microphones are double-edged swords. On the one hand, they make it possible for everyone to hear the person speaking. On the other hand, many people are very shy in front of a microphone, either electing not to share at all, or holding the microphone so far from their mouths that their voices are not picked up. If you need to use a microphone (i.e. because you are in a very large space), you may want to make it less intimidating by adding some of those colorful strips of paper rules to it, as in the first example, or wrapping a few fake flowers around it.

❑ **Use a beanbag or other object that is easy to throw and catch.** A talking piece works best when it is being handed to someone who is sitting right next to you. When it needs to be handed across the room, as in, when you are calling on groups that are sitting far apart from each other, it can become more of a nuisance than a help. Using an object designed for participants to toss to each other makes it easier to "pass the baton" and can be a lot of fun.

❑ **Keep track of the piece.** It is, unfortunately, fairly easy to continually call on the same small group of enthusiastic participants. These are the ones who eagerly raise their hands and feel comfortable speaking in front of large groups. One bonus outcome of using a talking piece is that you can be more mindful of who has had a turn with it. Before you call on someone and hand over the piece, take a moment to reflect on whether you've already given the piece to that person recently. If so, aim to hand it to someone who hasn't had a turn yet. If it is hard for you to keep track, you can distribute an equal number of items (e.g. two "tickets") to each participant and ask participants to give you one of the items when they receive the piece. Once they've used up their items, they must wait until everyone else has used theirs before they can hold the piece again.

Talking pieces can also be used during small group work time, or even in pair-shares if you bring in multiple pieces. As facilitator, you can watch the piece being passed and make sure that the conversation is moving from person to person, and isn't being dominated by one voice. In short, it provides you with a visual cue during these times of who is, and has been, speaking.

If you are not already using a talking piece in your engagements, I encourage you to try it out and see what a difference it can make in encouraging everyone to have their turn to share.

NOTES

CHAPTER 31

Let Them Share What They Already Know

The "Protégé Effect" is a well-researched phenomenon. What scientists have discovered, and what we, as Transformational Facilitators know, is that when a participant teaches the material, they learn it better.[23]

In addition to simply gaining a deeper understanding of the subject matter, designing your agenda so that participants teach each other empowers them in the precise way that we aim to do with Transformational Facilitation - by raising up participants so that everyone in the room is on equal footing.

Here are some ideas for how to create opportunities for participants to share what they already know about the topic at hand in your engagements.

❏ **Use a "KWL" chart.** In Chapter 27, I talk about using this strategy in your engagements. In the first step, the "K" asks participants to share what they already know about a topic. This is a great way to help them not only learn from each other, but also make connections between what they know and are about to cover.

❏ **Use a jigsaw.** I cover this method in more detail in Chapter 42. In this activity, participants each read a short section of a longer document, and then "teach" their peers about what they read.

❏ **Do role plays.** Provide a scenario to a pair of participants or small group. (For example, prior to starting peer-coaching, you can ask them to act out a peer coaching scene in which the coach is acting more like a lecturer than a coach). As they work through how they will solve the problem presented in the scenario, they are actually coming up with solutions that they are discussing and explaining to their peers. In short, they are teaching each other!

❏ **Set up peer coaching.** While the coaching process I explain in Chapter 23 is very explicit about making sure the coach is drawing out solutions from the coachee by asking questions, not offering answers, the process of supporting their peer serves to reinforce their own thoughts on the topic, so I am including it here in my list of strategies.

❏ **Let them give each other feedback.** As participants analyze a partners' ideas or strategy and then share their thoughts with that person/people, they are, in effect, teaching. When using this strategy, it is extremely important to reinforce how to offer constructive feedback, meaning, feedback that builds up ideas of what TO do, rather than focusing strictly on what NOT to do.

---

[23] (Koh et al.)

❑ **Give them opportunities to write.** Although it is not directly teaching, reflecting is a powerful form of self-teaching, particularly if you frame the question, "What do you know about the subject?" or "What did you learn about the topic?" You do not need to invite participants to share their writing out loud, although this is a strategy I cover in Chapter 50.

❑ **Let them take the stage.** Give small groups or pairs a topic or piece of a topic, allow them time to make a poster or prepare a short presentation/activity, and then let them get up in front and truly be the teacher. Use a timer and keep the stage time short (e.g. under three minutes), and encourage participants to use Transformational Facilitation strategies (or at least keep it fun) when possible.

❑ **Find co-facilitators.** This is my favorite strategy of all. When I have had the same person attend many of my workshops or meetings, I love to include them in facilitating the event. Depending on how much time and energy they can contribute to facilitation, we usually do an hour-long pre-planning meeting where we divide up roles and responsibilities within the agenda. There is nothing like actual experience up in front of the room!

As you create your next agenda, aim to include at least one agenda item that takes advantage of the Protégé Effect. Your participants will get more out of the engagement, and will feel empowered while doing so!

NOTES

SECTION FOUR
USE ACTIVE LEARNING AND ENGAGEMENT STRATEGIES

Andragogy is the study of adult learning, (just as "pedagogy" is the study of child-learning, as the root "peda" would suggest). Malcolm Knowles is considered one of the originators, and certainly is the most popular proponent of adult learning theory. The works of Howard Gardner and his theory of Multiple Intelligences and Carol Dweck on Growth Mindset are key ideas that are important to this section as well. I'm going to take a moment here to briefly outline these theories and how they relate to Transformational Facilitation.

Andragogy

Malcolm Knowles outlined a number assumptions about adult learners that are helpful to think about when preparing to carry out Transformational Facilitation.[24] As you read through this list, think about which of these are true for you, as an adult learner.

> → Adults are capable of directing (and want to direct) their own learning.
> → Adults have a lot of experience to draw on as they engage in learning new material.
> → Adults are more aware of the value of learning than children are.
> → Adults have practical reasons and motivations for wanting to learn (e.g. to be better at their jobs).
> → Adults want what they are learning to be immediately applicable.
> → Adults are internally motivated to learn and require less external motivation than children do.

Transformational Facilitation capitalizes on these assumptions by actively creating opportunities for adults to make choices, share their experience, and connect what they are experiencing to its practical applications.

Multiple Intelligences

For many people, Howard Gardner's theory[25] is now very familiar, the main idea being that each person has different ways of processing information and there is not just one type of intelligence. For many people, the idea of approaching information using a varied and creative toolbox of strategies based on this theory resonates and is helpful. While Gardner was focused on "intelligences" and not "learning styles," I am using his list here to encourage you to think about which of these you rely on most as you learn.

> → **Verbal-linguistic:** Do you like to analyze information through speaking and writing?
> → **Logical-mathematical:** Do you like looking for proofs or solving abstract problems?
> → **Visual-spatial:** Do you like creating maps and graphic representations?
> → **Musical:** Are you drawn to music and sound?
> → **Naturalistic:** Are you sensitive to and hold a great love for plants and animals?
> → **Bodily-kinesthetic:** Do you like to move your body to solve problems or make things?
> → **Interpersonal:** Are you easily able to understand other people?
> → **Intrapersonal:** Do you have a clear sense of self and your motivations and intentions?

---

[24] See (M. S. Knowles), (M. Knowles, *The Adult Learner*), and (M. Knowles, *Andragogy in Action*)
[25] See (Gardner)

Transformational Facilitation, and particularly the ideas in this section, draws on this theory as participants are encouraged to interact and engage using a wide range of the strategies mentioned above. As you read through the next section, notice how these intelligences are being put into play and how you can capitalize on them as you plan your agendas.

Growth Mindset

Growth Mindset belongs to a set of theories and practices known as "Social and Emotional Learning." These include all of those soft skills that people need to succeed, like the ability to work well with others, manage our emotions, work hard, etc. Carol Dweck's research[26] demonstrates that when people have a "growth mindset," they believe that anything can be learned or achieved with practice. With a growth mindset, we are better able to learn and persevere in the face of difficulty. With a fixed mindset, people believe that ability is fixed and no amount of work or practice or learning can change that. When in a fixed mindset, we are more likely to get frustrated, give up, or not even try to improve.

In what areas of your life or work do you have a "fixed" mindset?

_____

_____

In what areas of your life or work do you have a "growth" mindset?

_____

_____

_____

Transformational Facilitation accesses Dweck's theories as it attempts to put participants into a growth mindset, or, to put it another way, encourages a "can do" attitude.

As you read through this section, you may recognize other research and theories as well. Notice those connections as you think about how to keep the people you are working with active, engaged, and motivated to participate.

As you enter this section, reflect for a minute on the following questions:

What theories do I currently believe in or rely on in my work?

_____

_____

_____

What do I currently do to encourage active engagement with participants?

_____

_____

_____

What is my vision for full and active engagement of participants?

_____

_____

_____

---

[26] See (Dweck).

CHAPTER 32
Use Quotes

I saw a great bumper sticker the other day: "Compassion is not weakness, and concern for the unfortunate is not socialism." I looked it up, and it is attributed to Hubert H. Humphrey, a mid-20th century American politician who passed away in the mid 1970s.

I say it was "great" because in the two seconds that it took me to read it, I immediately felt a resounding "yes!" that lifted my spirits (stuck in traffic and brought down by the weight of the world as I tend to be). And that is the beauty of a good quote. It only takes a second to read and know if you agree.

Sometimes when I am having difficulty making decisions (e.g., do I want to go camping this weekend or not?), I flip a coin. Heads, I'll go camping. Tails, I'll stay home. I flip the coin and, aha! Heads! I am going camping! I immediately feel my heart sink. And then I know. Then I'm in touch. I really don't want to go camping. Decision done. I ignore the actual outcome of the coin toss for the far more valuable insight it gave me into my own feelings.

Using quotes in your workshops and meetings can have the same effect. It can help people get in touch with their thoughts on a subject in a way that is immediate and compelling. And, luckily for us, with sites like BrainyQuote.com, this resource is just a few clicks away.

Here is an example, in case you are wondering how quotes could be used.

1. Imagine you are running a workshop on... oh, I don't know, let's say Supervising Staff. Now I'm just going to type "Leadership" into Brainy-Quote, copy a couple of quotes...

→ "Leadership is not about a title or a designation. It's about impact, influence and inspiration. Impact involves getting results, influence is about spreading the passion you have for your work, and you have to inspire teammates and customers." Robin S. Sharma

→ "Leadership is a privilege to better the lives of others. It is not an opportunity to satisfy personal greed." Mwai Kibaki

→ "I know of no single formula for success. But over the years I have observed that some attributes of leadership are universal and are often about finding ways of encouraging people to combine their efforts, their talents, their insights, their enthusiasm and their inspiration to work together." Queen Elizabeth II

2. Now I will put each of these on an 8.5 x 11 inch piece of paper and tape it up on a wall of the room we are in. I will ask participants to read the quotes to themselves and then go stand by the one that "resonates" with them the strongest. You know, the one that makes them go, "Yes!"

3. Once they are grouped around their chosen quote, I will ask them to talk, as a group or with a partner, about why they selected that quote. Next I will ask them to discuss (with the same group or partner) how the quote they selected relates to their work supervising staff.

4. I'll then invite them to sit back down and ask for a few volunteers to share out what they heard their partner say about the quote they were standing near. This makes for a much richer conversation than if we had just started with, "Good supervisors do X" or even, "Discuss your supervision style with a partner." And, it doesn't take a whole lot of extra effort on your part as a facilitator, because those quotes are so easily found online.

So my challenge to you with this chapter is a pretty simple one: Use quotes in your next meeting or workshop to launch a conversation or topic and get everyone actively engaged. This activity can be done in ten minutes. It can work as an ice-breaker/warm up activity, as a "brain break" midway through an event, or even as a closing conversation.

Because, "When someone asks me to do something, something new, something I don't know about, and if I haven't done it, I'll say yes. Just so I can try something new. You never know what you might like." - Osric Chau

NOTES

CHAPTER 33
Keep Moving

You know something I really dislike about attending workshops and meetings? Sitting in a chair for hours on end. Even if the presenter is highly engaging and full of bright ideas, the act of sitting still and listening tries both my physical and mental patience.

And you know what? It's not just *physically* bad for us to sit for long stretches. Research shows that we actually think better when we are... yep, you guessed it, standing up.[27]

I like to follow a personal rule of not letting participants sit still for more than twenty to thirty minutes at a stretch, so a Transformational Facilitation strategy for you is to challenge yourself to do the same. How can you structure your up-coming meetings or workshops so that participants spend as much time on their feet as in their chair?

One note, if you have someone with mobility issues who will not be able to move around as described in the activities below, think about how you can incorporate other types of movement that the person can do, and/or how you can bring people to that person, so that they are not left on the sidelines sitting out of the activity.

If you're feeling overwhelmed with my challenge, here are a few simple ideas:

❑ **Start your session with an icebreaker that requires people to move around.** One of my favorites is a quick mingle-type activity. Here's how it works:

1. Invite participants to stand up, walk around the room and stand back to back with someone who is their "shoe partner," meaning, someone who has shoes that are similar (or opposite) to their own shoes. (I will go into more detail about "shoe partners" in the next chapter.) You could also ask people to stand back-to-back with someone who they've never talked with before, a birthday partner (same month, same year, same astrological sign), etc.

By the way, I ask people to stand back-to-back because it a) helps me see quickly who still needs a partner and b) keeps people from immediately starting to talk, which is harder to do when you are back-to-back.

2. Once everyone has a partner, introduce an opening question for discussion. Pairs should remain standing while they are talking to each other. Don't forget to remind them to first turn around and introduce themselves, especially if they don't already know each other! Discussion questions should be related to the topic(s) you are planning to cover in your engagement. So, if it was a workshop on facilitation, for example, I might ask the pairs to discuss the worst workshop they'd ever been to and what made it so horrible.

3. Repeat this process three times with three different questions, so that everyone has a chance to talk with three different partners and move around on three different occasions. It goes without saying (but I'm going to say it anyway),

---

[27] (Siddarth et al.)

that anyone with a physical need to sit should be allowed to do so! The point is to encourage movement, not make people uncomfortable.

❑ **Create opportunities to stand during the engagement.** I especially encourage this strategy during brainstorming. It's no surprise to me that research is now confirming something that I have often noticed: people are more engaged in discussions and generate better ideas when they are on their feet. Instead of asking people to shout out brainstorming ideas from their seats, post up a piece of chart paper on a wall and have small groups stand around the sheets as they write their ideas down using markers.

❑ **When all else fails, have people get up and stretch.** If you really, truly cannot come up with a way to have participants stand during your workshop, then the least you can do is lead everyone in a three-minute stretch break. Or, better yet, ask a participant to volunteer to lead the stretch activity!

❑ **Move to share.** After tables have completed an activity together (e.g., finished a discussion, read a document, written responses to a question), invite everyone to stand up and find someone from a different table to share what they learned. Of course, you could just as easily do this debrief sitting down at their tables, but in the interest of getting people up on their feet, encourage them to walk around and hold their conversations standing.

❑ **I always like to do my close-out standing up,** and usually in a circle. I really feel that people not only *think* better when they are standing up, but listen better to each other as well. As you hold your closing reflections, consider doing so, in whatever form it takes, with everyone on their feet. While I have in the past done a mingle, I find that the energy at the end of a workshop or meeting is often a little more mellow, so simply standing in a circle feels more comfortable - we are still up, but we are not running around.

What other ideas can you come up with for getting people up and moving?

_____

_____

_____

How can you integrate this into your agendas?

_____

_____

_____

CHAPTER 34
Switch Up Partners and Groups Often

At many of the engagements I lead, meeting and learning from new people is a high point for participants. While not everyone is there to network, being in a room together with a bunch of people who have gathered for a specific and shared purpose is powerful. If it were an online course, with each person in their own room at their own computer, I might not feel as compelled to create opportunities for people to meet and share with each other. But, when physically together in the same space, it seems like a wasted opportunity if I don't encourage them to interact with and get to know new people.

I also find that when people enter a room, they automatically sit down next to people they already know or talk with on a regular basis. While I respect and understand that choice, I also want to stretch people's comfort zone by creating opportunities for them to step away from that familiar group and lean out into a new space, where new ideas often await.

Here are a couple of ways you can shake things up and make it easy for participants to meet, talk with, and learn from new people, without simply asking people to count off or turn to the person next to them. Each time you create a new group or partnership, don't forget to remind people to introduce themselves to each other! If you don't say it explicitly, I have found that people often simply launch into their conversations having never learned their partner's name, role, or organization!

❑ One of my favorite ways to pair people is by asking them to find a "shoe partner." I actually usually start with this one because instead of having to walk around looking at people's faces, which can be uncomfortable in a room that hasn't warmed up yet, participants get to walk around looking down at the ground. A shoe partner is anyone whose shoes in some way match yours. Maybe they are the same color, same brand, same type, or maybe they are complete opposites (heels with boots).

❑ **Ask them to stand back to back.** As I mentioned in the previous chapter, I always ask participants to stand back-to-back with their partner once they have identified one. This helps give me a quick visual of who still needs a partner. It also makes it more difficult for people to launch into conversations, which is useful because I generally haven't given out the discussion prompt yet. It is easier to listen when you aren't directly facing someone you haven't really met yet!

❑ **Hand out cards.** Another fun way to pair people is with a deck of "Old Maid" cards, which are easy to find at the dollar store. Hand out the cards as participants enter the room, or leave them on the table at each seat. Now invite participants to try to find their match (and stand back-to-back once they have)! You can also use a regular deck of cards, and group people by number, suit, color, etc.

❑ **Use birthdays.** In a recent workshop I returned to another favorite, birthdays. In this method I ask participants to line up, without speaking, in order of their birthdays (not by year, just by month and day). We then went down the line to see if they got it right. From here you can either have people turn to someone next to them, or create small groups. I like to joke with participants that they are now working with people from the same or nearby astrological sign, and we shall see if that has any effect on their conversations.

❑ **Ask them to find a brand new partner.** I also love asking participants, particularly near the end of a workshop or event, to find someone they haven't yet met or talked with. At this point, walking around and actually picking a partner feels a lot more comfortable to people than it did in the beginning of our time together, and they usually find their pairings quickly.

Go deeper. When forming small groups that will be working with each other for a while, I like to give them a little more time to get to know each other than simply quick introductions. After they go around sharing their names, jobs, and where they work (if they don't already work together), you can ask them to share why they are at the event, what they hope to get out of the day, or some other similar prompt. Now ask them to create a "team name" for themselves, since they will be working together for the next thirty minutes. I invite groups to share their team names and why they chose those names, then give each team a special cheer. Taking the time to build a little group cohesion after having formed these new groups goes a long way in making the following activity or agenda item more fun.

While participants may be resistant at first, I strongly encourage you to create your agenda with an opportunity to chat with someone new at least every thirty minutes and take advantage of everyone being in the room together.

CHAPTER 35
Use Turn-and-Talks or Pair-Shares

As we have seen, one concept that repeats itself throughout Transformational Facilitation is the idea that participant voices matter. Not just that their opinions and ideas matter; but that actually speaking, using their voice, matters. Here's a mindfulness exercise to try: Set a timer for one minute. Close your eyes. Now as you sit quietly, listen to the sounds around you. What do you hear? If you did this during a typical meeting or workshop you attend or lead, what would you hear?

We may not always be aware of it, but, as facilitators, we often talk too much. Our voices become the central tone in the room. Or, to think of it in musical terms, we become the "key signature." And, while we definitely want there to be a tone of positive, empowering words and ideas, we don't need it to be *our* tone. Rather, we need to ask, how can we fill the room with participant tones and voices? (In fact, I have a dream of doing a "talk audit" in my engagements, where I record the entire meeting or workshop, and then record how many minutes I am talking versus how many minutes each participant is talking. I haven't done it yet, but will let you know when I do!)

So, with this in mind, one of the ideas you will see repeated throughout these chapters is what I refer to as a "pair-share," often called "turn and talk," "partner sharing," etc. The main idea is that partners discuss a prompt with each other. They are then often (but not always) asked to share out what they heard their partner say with a larger group or the whole group.

Every time you use a turn and talk, you are inviting everyone's voices into the room. While it is true that occasionally in a partnership one person will do all of the talking, if you make the time limit clear and even tell people when it is time to switch which partner is sharing, by the end of the activity, everyone's voice has had a chance to be heard by someone in the room.

This matters. Not just because you want to decrease your own voice, but because this is how people learn. In fact, research has shown that when we have a chance to express our ideas out loud, ***even if no one is listening***, we can learn almost three times more than when we don't voice our thoughts out loud.[28] Let that sink in for a minute.

So, if we, as facilitators, are the central tone in the room and the ones doing most of the talking, who is doing most of the thinking and learning?

Here is my challenge to you for this chapter: Do a turn and talk during your next engagement. At least once. After you present a piece of information, ask participants to turn to the person next to them and discuss:

> → How is this information relevant to you?
> → What has your experience with this been?
> → How might you apply this to your work?

---

[28] (Boser, "Talking to Yourself (Out Loud) Can Help You Learn") (Boser, *Learn Better*)

And give it enough time! Set a timer for at least three to five minutes (or longer if you can) and let people really have a turn to put their voices out there.

For more ideas on questions you can ask to get dialogue going, visit Chapter 46. Try this strategy out and see how it goes. I bet you will be pleasantly surprised by the results!

NOTES

CHAPTER 36
Share Research and Evidence

I have to be honest. I love research. Especially when it underscores and validates what I already, in my heart, know to be true. I also love research that opens up my eyes to something I had never considered before. That feeling of shock (I had no idea!) is fun and makes my brain light up.

Using research in your facilitation is also important because it can help participants understand the *why*. As in, this is why we are proposing this solution. Or this is why we are encouraging you to try this strategy.

So, of course, the question becomes, how do you integrate research into your workshops and meetings in a way that helps participants feel inspired and motivated by what is being shared? Here are a couple of suggestions to get you started:

❏ **Choose the right research.** It may seem obvious, but choosing research that is not quite in line with the point you are trying to make can do more damage than good, as it can confuse participants. Look at a couple of different pieces of research on the topic you will be covering to make sure you have found the most relevant one.

❏ **Make sure the research you are bringing is valid and from a trusted source.** This should go without saying, but there is a lot of junk out there, especially on the internet. Just because someone had an experience of something (I'm looking at you, Ted Talks*), doesn't mean it's universally true. Sometimes older research has been disproven, or added to. Look for research from universities, or that has been published in credible academic publications. In short, do a little research about your research.

❏ **Consider the format.** I have used direct pages from published research, but sometimes using a newspaper or magazine article *about* the research is easier to digest, as the key points are usually distilled and it may be written in less obtuse academic language. You can also often find videos of researchers talking about their work. These clips can be a great way to introduce your participants to both the research and the researcher.

❏ **Plan how participants will engage with the information.** To make the use of research Transformational, you will need to think creatively about how you are introducing it. For ideas on how to do this, see Chapter 42.

❏ **Encourage participants to find and bring in related research.** Not only is this Transformative in that participants are contributing to the content of the engagement, it is a chance for you and your group to synthesize the material and the topic you are covering. If the research they bring in adds to the body of knowledge, then you know people are on the right track. If the research they bring in is off-topic or irrelevant, then you know you need to do more work to clarify your point.

Try bringing some research into your next meeting or workshop and notice what it does for your group!

* A Ted Talk video clip can be a welcome addition to your engagement, just be mindful of the difference between personal testimony and research.

NOTES

CHAPTER 37
Use Video Clips

Video clips can be a great way to introduce information or illustrate concepts during a workshop or meeting. Here are a few tips, tricks, and ideas to get you thinking about how, when, or whether to use videos in your meetings or workshops.

❑ **Triple check to make sure everything is working.** Beyond the issues you have with PowerPoint presentations, with video you also have to make sure the sound is working, and, if you are using a YouTube or Vimeo clip, that the internet connection is good enough. Nothing like a silent or stalled video to waste precious time and lose participant focus. As much as possible, download video clips to your laptop (rather than streaming them via internet), and bring spare speakers.

❑ **Make a "Plan B."** Because things often go wrong, be prepared with a backup plan if the video won't play. Transcripts, screen captures, alternative activities - make sure you have something so that all is not lost when the video doesn't work (because I have seen this happen all too often and it can really derail the event).

❑ **Choose your clips wisely.** If you only need a piece of the whole to make your point, then only show that piece. No need to waste time watching fifteen minutes when the key points are covered in the first three minutes. When in doubt, go short to maximize everyone's attention span.

❑ **Use your own clips.** This works really well if you are trying to demonstrate something you'd like your participants to analyze; for example, a teacher teaching a classroom lesson, a facilitator running a meeting, or an interaction between two customers. Using your own clips can be very powerful and only requires a smartphone. Again, keep it short (no need to watch the entire lesson, just the parts you'd like participants to focus on).

❑ **Choose two different clips and then ask participants to discuss the similarities/differences.** As an example, you could show two different facilitators running a meeting, two different staff members interacting with customers, or two different advertisements for similar products. This can really generate some lively discussion and can be very useful for raising key points.

❑ **Pose questions prior to viewing.** By doing this, participants are watching with a purpose. Likewise, pause the video at intervals (especially longer videos) and provide prompts for pairs or small groups to discuss. I cover this in much greater depth in Chapter 42.

❑ **If your group meets regularly, ask them to bring in video clips**, either that they have recorded themselves or that they find online, that illustrate a point you are learning about or covering. These can be shared, compared, and discussed and have the added value of putting the power and learning back into the hands of participants. Be clear about the format you will need, or better yet, ask them to send them in in advance so you can make sure they all work.

❑ **Think outside the box.** Sometimes clips from cartoons or sitcoms illustrate a point as well or even better than a recorded lecture by a professor or a TED talk. Plus, they have the added value of being entertaining and the non-direct connection will force participants to think even harder. Challenge yourself to do this next time you are considering using video!

❑ **Videos can be used at any point during an engagement.** They can launch an opening discussion to set the stage for the day's topic, be used to deliver content throughout the meeting, or generate a closing inspiration when used toward the end of a session. The important thing is to check the ebb and flow of your agenda, as they require quiet sitting and listening, and are best preceded and followed by a more active activity (e.g. a discussion, mingling, or group activity).

I, myself, tend to shy away from using video because of the technological issues and the work it takes to get everything set up. However, as I challenge you to integrate video in meaningful ways into your engagements, I'll challenge myself to do the same.

CHAPTER 38
Represent Ideas Visually

Much has been written over the years about the benefits of including visuals in facilitation. [29] In fact, a whole field called "Graphic Facilitation," exists, complete with books, online resources, and workshops you can attend to learn how to use visual strategies in your work. Perhaps you've even had the pleasure of attending an event that includes a "graphic recorder," who creates a mural-map of the event in real time. It is very helpful and I encourage you to seek out those resources if that is something you are excited to pursue.

What I am going to talk about, however, is how I incorporate activities that require *participants* to generate visuals. I am trained both as a visual artist and an art teacher, and it is almost impossible for me to lead a workshop or meeting that doesn't, at some point, require participants to do some sort of art-making. As I like to say, "art is a way of thinking." What I mean by this is that when we talk or write, we are only accessing one part of our brains. The minute we are asked to create something artistic, it lights up a whole other side of our thinking.

In fact, there is a body of research that points to how much better we learn when art is included, as in a recent study[30] which demonstrates that drawing about a concept is more effective in helping to remember it than reading or writing about it is.

In addition, when fun, hands-on activities are included in your agenda, people are able to relax and enjoy the process, especially since it is so often outside of what people are accustomed to doing. This breath of fresh air allows everyone to think more freely and creatively. If you are not already incorporating arts-based activities into your agendas, I encourage you to try it, even if you don't feel confident in your artistic abilities.

Here are a few ideas to get you started:

- ❑ **Steer clear of drawing, at first.** If you are nervous about including visual representation into your events, one reason might be because you feel you lack the ability to draw. This, unfortunately, is true for many people, and often asking them to draw can make them freeze up or get very uncomfortable. To get around this, bring in magazines, and let them cut out and glue pictures to create collages instead. Some collage ideas include:

  → A self-portrait (participants can cut out both words and images for this) to be used as part of an icebreaker
  → A timeline of a project, where participants find images that represent various stages of individual or group projects they are working on
  → A problem you are working to address with clients, in which participants create a visual representation of something they/their clients are struggling with

---

[29] (Amit et al.)
[30] (Fernandes et al.)

❑ In group projects, let each group **select one person to be the "artist."** I find that an eager artist always surfaces within each group. This person is given the marker and paper and charged with representing the ideas of their group, on behalf of their group mates. Some ways to incorporate a group artist might be:

> → Create a picture of a great staff member. What skills and abilities does that person have?
> → Draw a map of our organization and stake-holders. Who and where are we?
> → Outline your vision for our department in the next five years. Where will we be?

❑ **Provide a template**. Handing out an already-started graphic helps people get started in thinking visually. Instead of having to start from scratch, they have a map to fill in and get them rolling. Some ways to include graphic organizers are:

> → Thought bubbles. You can put a person or a light bulb in the center of the page with thought bubbles radiating out. People fill the bubbles with drawings or words related to the topic you are covering or a prompt you give.
> → Half a thing (e.g. a horse, house, truck, etc.). People fill in the other half with something else, like wheels for the horse, wings for the house, or people in the truck. Partners discuss what they chose to add to the object, what it creates, and how it relates to the topic at hand (this is where the creative thinking really kicks in!).
> → Decorate it. Have participants trace, or provide an outline of, a hand, or other object, and invite participants to decorate it with images, doodles, and words that relate to your topic. This can be an activity, or simply left on tables like coloring pages.

❑ **Make it 3-D.** To really get those creative juices going, bring in playdough, toilet paper tubes, newspaper, tape, pieces of cardboard - you name it - and let people go to town creating. Some things you could ask them to create include:

> → A bridge that can actually hold weight, (with a silly prize for the group whose bridge can hold the most weight), or a tower (again, with a prize for the tallest one).
> → A model of your organization. Let each group explain their model to the other groups when they are finished.
> → An "invention" that would address a problem participants experience re-gularly.
> → An animal with qualities that represent your organization (or a hybrid animal!).

I understand that incorporating art activities into your agenda may seem like it will take too much time, make too much of a mess, or make you feel uncomfortable. I encourage you to push yourself and make it happen anyway. I have seen full rooms of people with low or even negative energy get completely turned around into energetic and enthusiastic participants when they are asked to tackle a creative challenge. Try it and notice what happens!

CHAPTER 39
Sort Notes

As Dave Gray, Sunni Brown, and James Macanufo point out in their book, Gamestorming, "[Humans] are so good at finding patterns that once we find one, it can be difficult to see anything else."[31] If we want participants to break out of old ways of thinking and bring out new ideas (which we do as Transformational Facilitators!), we need to help people see new patterns, instead of defaulting back to what they already/always see.

One of the simplest ways to shake up people's thinking, and therefore encourage everyone to let NEW patterns emerge, is to put their ideas onto moveable objects: sticky notes, index cards, anything that can be arranged and rearranged in multiple ways.

So here's your challenge for this chapter: The next time you do a brainstorming session, instead of charting everyone's responses on a large white-board or chart paper, have everyone write their ideas down on sticky notes (if it's large group, I often use the half-sheet sized stickies (e.g. 4" x 6"), or, if you are familiar with ToP (Technology of Participation), you can use a Sticky Wall, which is super fun and convenient!).[32]

Once people have had time to generate their ideas, writing down one idea per sticky note, there are endless things you can do with them.

Here's an example: I ask participants to brainstorm what makes a good leader. They are each given ten sticky notes for their brainstorm. I have a couple of options now. This is where it really starts to get fun! Depending on your space, you can do this on a wall, on a table, or even on the floor.

- ❑ Ask them to get into groups of four, so that each group has forty sticky notes, and see if they can sort their notes by putting similar concepts together until all of the notes are in a category.

- ❑ Post categories around the room (in this instance those might be something like, "Inter-personal," Intrapersonal," "Microlevel" and "Macrolevel") and ask participants to try to sort their notes into those categories.

- ❑ Ask people to take turns posting their ideas up one at a time. As someone posts an idea, anyone who has a similar idea can put their sticky note up with the one that is already posted and explain why they think the two go together.

- ❑ Ask everyone to put all of their sticky notes on a table, and then invite people to walk around and collect five sticky notes that they feel are most important in a good leader and post those up together.

---

[31] (Gray et al.)

[32] A Sticky Wall is a large sheet with a tacky surface that allows you to stick, move, and restick papers or index cards to it. It is a great alternative to using Sticky Notes because you can use any sized paper. See https://www.ica-usa.org/store.html

❑ Ask people to post them all up and then pick three that they feel they possess already as a leader, and three that they feel they still need to work on.

As you are probably realizing now, there are dozens (hundreds?) of activities you can do with those notes! I've left some brainstorming space below for you to generate ideas for when/what/how to use this concept.

If you are familiar with Spark Decks, you know that our cards fill a similar purpose. Rather than publishing a curriculum or handbook for staff to walk through, the use of a deck, which can be sorted and organized in any order, breaks up the linear thinking (and groaning) that can sometimes accompany a bound text.

If you like this chapter, you'll love gamestorming.com. It is a great library of fun ways to get your group into brainstorming mode.

CHAPTER 40
Use Venn Diagrams

I incorporate a lot of common teaching strategies into my facilitation work with adults simply because they work. A Venn diagram is a perfect example of this. At its heart, the purpose of a Venn diagram is to help users visualize similarities and differences between two entities. Here are a couple of examples of ways to use Venn diagrams in a workshop or meeting that support fun, interactive learning and deeper engagement with information.

❑ **As an icebreaker.** Pair participants and give each pair a blank Venn diagram. Ask them to write their names in the outer circles and then list out eight to ten unique characteristics about themselves in the outer circles while finding eight to ten things they have in common for the inner circle. Go around the room and have pairs introduce each other by sharing their partner's name and one thing that is different about themselves and their partner and one thing that is similar about themselves and their partner based on their diagram.

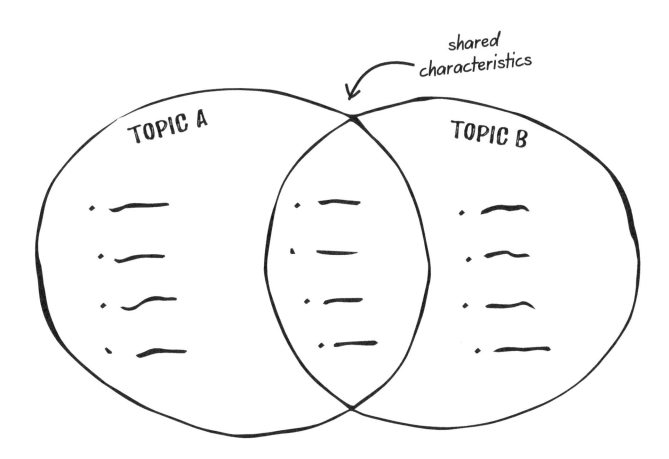

❑ **When evaluating options.** Say you are considering two or three locations for an upcoming fundraiser. Before evaluating the options, help everyone get on the same page by listing out all of the similarities and differences between the two or more venues using a Venn diagram. This can make coming to a decision a lot easier.

❑ **As a team builder.** One activity I've done a number of times is create groups and give each group a diagram with two different animals listed (e.g. tiger and snake, horse and beetle, shark and cat, etc.). Groups complete the Venn diagram by writing the similarities between the two animals in the place where the two circles overlap, and their differences in the outer part of the circles. Next, each member of the group is given a blank sheet of paper and crayons/markers to create a drawing of the new, hybrid animal based on the shared characteristics from the section of the diagram where the circles overlap. Now go around the room and have each group show their drawings. Can the other groups guess which two animals the hybrid is of? This is a lot of fun and the resulting name (a hybrid mashup of the two animal names), can be used as the group's name or mascot, if the group will continue working together during the session.

❑ **As a way to analyze new information.** Comparing old ideas to new ideas can help participants make the leap to doing things a new way. For example, you could put "last year's staff retreat" on one side of the Venn diagram, and "this year's staff retreat," which hasn't happened yet, on the other side. Now ask pairs to list out what will be the same and different about the two retreats using the diagram. Now ask the partners to join another pair of participants, discuss what they wrote, and collectively come up with five key changes for "this year's staff retreat" that they then share with the whole group.

❑ **In personal action planning.** If you are covering a new way of doing things, for example, let's say you are going to cover healthier eating habits, a Venn diagram can be helpful. Ask participants to write down "my current eating habits," on one side of the circle before you start the workshop. At the end of the workshop, have them write what they learned on the other side of the circle labeled, "healthy eating habits." In the middle, they can now list out what is the same about how they've been eating, versus healthier eating. These become the lowest hanging fruit (pun intended) in their action planning, which I cover in Chapter 45.

Now it's your turn to come up with lots more creative ideas for how to incorporate Venn diagrams into your engagements. There are many other visual organizers out there, but this one is a good place to start as it is fairly simple and many people have used them before (in science class!), so they are familiar. They are also super versatile, so think outside the box (pun intended, again), and aim to incorporate a Venn diagram into your next engagement.

CHAPTER 41
Host a Gallery Walk

I often wonder who came up with the idea of a "museum." You know, where you walk from artwork to artwork around a room, looking at the pieces, reading the placard, absorbing the ambiance. Getting tired "museum feet."

I remember being dragged through art museums as a kid thinking it was the most boring thing in the world. When I really drill down into why I found it so tedious, I realize that it probably has something to do with the lack of interactivity in those endless white walls of art. Because now, when I drag my kids to a museum, there always seems to be some fun activity book to go along with the exhibits: scavenger hunts, blank pages to copy artworks, questions to answer. Someone figured out that simply looking at the art wasn't quite engaging enough for the average viewer like me.

You may, therefore, find it surprising that one of my favorite brainstorming activities is called "A Gallery Walk." The reason I love this activity, however, is because it is not only about VIEWING the gallery (yawn), but is also about CREATING it along the way (fun!).

Here's how it works:

1. Generate a list of questions or categories for which you want your group to brainstorm ideas. For example, if you are planning to host a school carnival, your categories might be:

> → Food
> → Entertainment
> → Activities for children ages 0-5
> → Activities for children ages 6-10?

Or, if you want your group to think about, say, making your organization a more "friendly" place for your clients, your categories might be questions like:

> → How is our building welcoming to people?
> → How do we show our clients that we care?
> → What is one thing you've seen a colleague do to make someone feel comfortable here?

2. Once you have your list of three to seven questions or categories, write each one at the top of a large sheet of chart paper, leaving a large blank space under this title. Hang these papers on the walls around the room, like a gallery.

3. Divide your group into pairs, triads, or small groups. You should have the same number of groups as there are papers on the wall. Give each group a marker and give them time to brainstorm on one of the papers, writing down their ideas in response to the question or category at the top of the paper.

4. After a few minutes, invite the groups to rotate to the next paper. Now they can read what the previous group wrote before adding their own responses to the brainstorm.

5. Continue until each group has had a chance to visit each poster.

6. At the end of this brainstorming session, I now like to ask participants to do any/all of the following:

> → Return to your original poster, read all of the ideas, and circle your favorite. Be prepared to share this idea out with the rest of the group along with *why* this idea was your favorite.
>
> → Walk around to view all of the posters and put a star by any ideas on any of the posters that jump out at you. Once this has been done, note if certain ideas got a lot of stars. Why do people think that is?
>
> → Walk around to all of the posters to read them. Now find a partner and discuss any themes or trends you notice across posters.
>
> → Read all of the posters and be prepared to ask a question about something you see, maybe something you don't understand, or something that requires more information.

7. After a group has done a gallery walk, I always type up the ideas and add them to our notes. Often, I will bring them back to our subsequent gathering and use them for another activity, like to form committees for the carnival in the first example above. There are many uses for ideas generated in a brainstorm like this.

Of course, it goes without saying that this type of brainstorming gets right at the heart of Transformational Facilitation because it really does generate full participation from everyone. If I just put up a chart paper in the front of the room and start asking people to brainstorm ideas for our school carnival, I will not get nearly the excitement and richness of response that I get when people are walking around the room writing their thoughts down in our gallery. And it necessitates interaction after the sheets have been filled in ways that are both thought-provoking and leaning towards action.

If you haven't tried doing a Gallery Walk before, try it. You will see how much more energy this generates when it's time to brainstorm. And if someone complains of "museum feet," by all means, let them pull up a chair to each paper.

CHAPTER 42
Make Information Accessible

Sometimes we just really want to "teach" something. What I mean by "teach" is that there is some critical piece of new information we really want to share. Since we don't want to lecture our participants, we often look to a video or article to do the lecturing for us. Now, knowing that lecturing is antithetical to Transformational Facilitation, here are some thoughts on how to keep those articles and videos from becoming veiled lectures.

❏ Before you begin, prepare and share a list of questions you'd like participants to keep in mind as they watch the video or read the article. For example, I may ask:

> → What is something that surprises you as you read?
> → What do you notice about the children in the video?
> → Where do you see yourself in this piece?

❏ Similarly, you can run this "scavenger hunt" style, where participants are asked to look for specific pieces of information. "The items for the hunt can either be closed (meaning, they only have one right response, as in the last question in the list below), or open (in that everyone in the room will come up with different answers).

> → Underline any points the author makes that you agree with.
> → Find three points in the video where you would do something differently.
> → What are the four main phases of the method?

❏ In both of the examples above, a guiding handout, with spaces for participants to write or take notes, is also helpful.

❏ Divide participants into small groups and have each group read and discuss a different paragraph of the article or watch a different video. Now have participants in each group count off one, two, three and then have all of the ones get together, etc., so that you have new groups, each of which has one member from the original groups. Members now explain to each other the part of the article they read or video they watched, so that participants are retelling and explaining to each other what they watched/read, (this is commonly called a "jigsaw").

❏ Pause the video at intervals, or break the article up by circling/numbering paragraphs and hold short pair-share or small group discussions to allow participants to process information as you move through it, and once it's finished. There are several types of prompting questions you can use for this, based on Bloom's Taxonomy;[33] they include:

✶ **Descriptive or basic comprehension questions**: Questions that start with who, what, where, when and ask participants to clarify what they saw/read or summarize/retell. This is the type of question I would use in the jigsaw example above. The purpose here is to make sure everyone understands the basic content.

---

[33] (Bloom)

> → What did you see the teacher doing?
> → Were there consistent words or phrases you heard used throughout the video?
> → Who was the article about?

* **Application questions**: These questions invite participants to apply what they just read/watched to something else, for example,

> → How is this similar to your experience?
> → How is this related to the topic we are covering today?
> → Why is this research important to your work?

* **Analysis questions**: These questions ask participants to break out concepts or ideas found in the article/video, for example,

> → How do the key features of the system the author is describing work together?
> → What evidence does the video show for why the method works?
> → How does this compare to the article we read earlier today?

* **Synthesis questions**: These ask participants to generate new ideas from what they just learned, for example,

> → How might you make changes in your practice based on what you learned from this article?
> → What other thoughts/questions does this video inspire in you?
> → What else would you add to this?

* **Evaluation questions**: These questions ask participants to form judgements about what they read or heard, as in,

> → Did you agree with the author, why or why not?
> → Do you think the method in the video worked, how?
> → What did you appreciate about what the article was suggesting?

Use this space to think about an upcoming meeting, class, workshop, or event you will be facilitating:

What video or article could you bring in to help participants engage with new content?

_____

_____

How can you introduce the content in an interactive way?

_____

_____

What questions could you ask participants to think about before, during, and after they view the video or read the article?

_____

_____

CHAPTER 43
Incorporate Reflection

I cannot emphasize strongly enough the power of reflection. Structured reflection helps participants connect theory and information with their personal experience and make it actually usable. [34] In fact, research in adult workplace learning shows that efforts are most effective when participants are able to self-regulate their learning by being in control of what they learn and evaluating their own progress, [35] and reflection is a key component of that regulation.

What follows in this chapter is a cycle of reflection that I really recommend you consider trying out. Responses to these questions can be in writing, in pair sharing, or even in small groups if participants feel comfortable with each other. At Spark Decks, we even supply a reflection Notebook that participants use throughout the engagement (and after the engagement is over), so you may want to consider providing a notebook or journal pages to help participants keep track of their thoughts and learning along the way.

Our process has four "phases." During each phase, we ask a different type of reflection question, and the responses to each type of question help scaffold and support the next question, meaning, it is helpful to ask the questions in the order outlined below. [36]

1. **Questions that help participants identify the current situation/issue.** Begin by inviting reflection that helps participants identify issues

they are facing or gaps in their knowledge or abilities. I generally ask these types of questions toward the beginning of the engagement once I have clarified the exact topic we are covering, but you could even do this prior to the meeting/workshop!

Here are some questions you might ask:

> → What is happening now (what, where, when, who, how much, how often)?
> → What is happening to YOU?
> → What is happening to others?
> → What are the effects of this?
> → What is missing in this situation? What do you need?
> → What do you think is the underlying cause of the issue?
> → What would you like to happen that is not happening now?
> → What would you like **not** to happen that is happening now?
> → What do you want to achieve long term?
> → What would be a short-term milestone along the way?
> → How will you know you've achieved your goal?
> → Is your goal attainable? Why or why not?

---

[34] (McCrindle and Christensen)
[35] (Milligan et al.)
[36] Our phases draw from many sources, including the ORID method (developed by the Institute for Cultural Affairs), and the GROW framework for coaching.

2. **Questions that help participants process how the information being shared relates to their situation.** Next, throughout the meeting or workshop, pause to allow time for participants to process what they have heard or done via open-ended questions. The purpose here is to help participants make decisions about potential efforts.

Here are some example questions:

> → In what ways does this relate to your experience?
> → What have you already done/tried related to this?
> → What else do you think you could try? What is still missing?
> → What would work about this option/strategy/suggestion?
> → What might be hard about this option/strategy/suggestion?
> → What have you seen work in similar circumstances or in the past?

3. **Questions that encourage participants to evaluate which information/learnings are be most beneficial to their situation.** Towards the end of the engagement, invite participants to reflect on the bigger picture of what they are taking away from the meeting/workshop and the next steps they plan to take or strategies they will try out. This is especially fun to do as a mingle activity, where participants get to chat with several different partners and really work out their ideas before sitting down to write them out on paper. I find that doing it this way also really gets everyone's energy up about taking action, which is the ultimate goal.

Some questions to prompt this could include:

> → Which options do you think will be most successful?
> → Why do you think that option will work?
> → What are you most excited about trying?
> → Which options do you plan to try and when?
> → Do these options address the underlying issues related to your needs? How?

4. **Questions that support participants to "learn by doing" after the engagement has ended.** Lastly, I work really hard to make sure that participants continue to learn and reflect after their time with me. That is where the true learning happens. As I mentioned above, we do this by providing everyone with a Notebook that has spaces for them to continually reflect.

Here are some post-engagement questions to encourage people to reflect on:

> → What strategies did you try and why?
> → What worked about the strategy?
> → What didn't work well about the strategy?
> → How would you modify the strategy so that it would work better next time?
> → What did you learn through trying out this strategy?

Even if you don't end up following such a structured use of reflection questions, I encourage you to try out including a few open-ended questions throughout your next event that offer participants an opportunity to consider their own reactions and place within the content. I think you will find that participants get a whole lot more out of the session when given an opportunity to reflect.

CHAPTER 44
Model for Participants
Modeling "Think Sheet"

I love the ideas Marie Kondo shares in her book (now a Netflix show!), *The Life-Changing Magic of Tidying Up.* [37] At least, I do in theory.

I read her book while my family and I were living in China. In China, it was an easy idea to absorb, because we had arrived there with only the allowable number of suitcases. We did not bring our five boxes of DVDs and CDs, our closets filled with favorite t-shirts from our youth, nor our piles of photo albums and books. Mostly, actually, our suitcases were filled with gifts that we planned to give to our new friends, refilling the empty suitcase space with souvenirs we knew we would collect along the way.

When I returned to the U.S., I was excited to start KonMari-ing my existence. After all, I had just spent a year living with more or less only the contents of a suitcase. Instead of unpacking my boxes of clothing from storage, I sorted them, only returning the items that "sparked joy" to my closet. The rest went straight to Goodwill. Same with my books, kitchenware, etc. It was a perfect time to declutter.

Until I couldn't find a pair of dress pants. Because the unfortunate truth is that while none of my dress pants had apparently sparked joy, I still needed a pair (or five) to wear to work.

Marie Kondo is not kidding about her strategy being "life-changing." The bigger idea in her decluttering philosophy is that by learning to unburden yourself of too many possessions, you will learn how to reconnect with what you value and to let go of that which is cluttering your life emotionally, like your bad marriage, lifeless job, or toxic friendships. It is not just about getting rid of the physical elements that are weighing you down, but ALL elements that are taking up too much space.

When we moved to China, one of the things I quickly noticed was how much free time we had. Why? Because we did not have a calendar packed with playdates, events, and obligations. Weekend days became long walks to long bus rides to accomplish a small task, like finding a bike helmet, an activity that in the States would have taken 30 minutes squashed between five or six other tasks and events. I absolutely loved all of this new-found leisure time. It was something I wanted to bring back with me to my previously hectic life in the U.S. How could I eliminate the busy-ness that had filled my life? Would it be possible to declutter my life in this way?

As for the dress pants, was the fact that I got rid of them all a sign of something greater? I began to ponder whether it was a call to a profession that did not require the wearing of dress pants.

Thus began my gradual shift toward a life that would allow me to wear fewer dress pants - and give me more free time. A far-away dream it seemed, but if I was going to experience some life-changing magic, at least I now had a goal to work toward. My year in China gave me the opportunity

---
[37] (Kondō)

to feel what life COULD be like if I possessed less and did less, and I loved it.

And you know what else I love? Running workshops. For me, it truly sparks joy. Perhaps because of this, one of the things I most enjoy doing in the workshops I run is modeling my methods. Particularly when I am facilitating workshops on the topic of Facilitation (which I often do!), and people are so clearly and deeply engaged and enjoying what we are doing, I will pause to ask participants, "What did you see me do during this activity?" or "Why do you think I chose to run this activity the way it was run?" When given a few minutes to reflect, participants will come up with a laundry list of strategies and ideas for how to improve facilitation so that it is more effective, fun, and engaging. I am not just *talking* about Transformational Facilitation, I am living it. And not only am I living it, I am making it transparent to the people experiencing it with me. *Not by telling them how to do it, but by showing them and allowing them to feel it happening.* And THIS BRINGS ME JOY.

I am sure you have noticed it yourself. Think about it for a minute. Can you recall the energy and vibrancy of a room where everyone is passionate about the topic at hand? Where the person facilitating is right in the water with you? Where you feel connected to those around you and lit up with new ideas?

Why wouldn't someone want to recreate that scenario? Because when given the tools, anyone can.

But, all too often, I see the person facilitating NOT modeling what it could be like. NOT walking the walk. I will never forget attending a conference where a panel of "experts" were lecturing a room packed with attendees on the topic of "the importance of interactive engagement." The irony was both laughable and infuriating. Really? You are going to "teach" me how to be *interactive* by lecturing at me from a stage?

What I find so valuable in Marie Kondo's method is not just that she forces you to sit with an object and notice how it makes you feel, but that she takes it one step further. Not only does she offer a tool to help you reconnect with your passions (answering the question, "Does this spark joy?"), she emboldens you to trust those feelings and toss out whatever *isn't* sparking joy.

So that is my Transformational Facilitation challenge for you in this chapter. I so often see my clients' calendars packed with meetings that take far too long, back to back to back. In those meeting rooms I see time wasted in passionless discussions that probably don't merit the two-hour window they've been given. I see the suck of energy that all of this meeting clutter has on people who are truly passionate about the causes they work for. It's time to think about moving away from that and toward engagements that bring everyone joy.

How?

- ❑ If you are a facilitator, I encourage you to start modeling. Model the transformational strategies that are in this book, like reducing lectures and increasing air time for participants, managing meeting time, and empowering participants to take action. Make the experience interactive and joyful.

- ❑ If you are someone whose calendar is packed, whose meetings and other "obligations" are withering your passion, toss those things out. Start with the low-hanging fruit; for KonMarie this is socks and underwear, for you this may be saying "no" to meetings that don't directly relate to your job, or cutting down scheduled meetings by thirty minutes, or looking for ways to authentically connect more during those meeting times.

I am by no means a poster child for KonMarie. The books and dishes and stuffed closets are still threatening to topple me at any moment, but the deeper lesson has stuck with me. While I will continue to work to master the material manifestation of the *Life-Changing Magic of Tidying Up*, I am grateful that I have the opportunity to use and share the Life-Changing Magic of Transformational Facilitation.

SECTION FIVE
MOTIVATE ACTION AND HELP PARTICIPANTS BRING IT BACK

As I mention in Section Four, adult learning theory posits that adults are more likely to be intrinsically motivated than children are.[38] But we have all had the experience of a colleague, coworker, classmate, or supervisee who just doesn't seem motivated to take on leadership, follow through on tasks, or learn new things. We might call it "burnout," "laziness," or "dispassion," but it all has the same feeling of drain, exhaustion, and sometimes even resistance.

There are many ways to address this challenge, and if you are running an organization, class, or program, you have probably used some or all of the following to motivate your students, employees, volunteers, etc:

> → Incentives
> → Coaching
> → Reorganization/Promotion
> → Grades
> → Degrees
> → Certificates
> → Wage increases
> →
> →

But many of the strategies we try out and use, like those outlined above, are external motivators. And we know from the research that external motivators are shaky, because once they are gone, people often revert to their previous behaviors.[39]

This is where Transformational Facilitation swoops in to steal the show. While all of the methods we covered in the previous chapters are pointed at building people's internal motivation, the chapters in this last section are specifically aimed at supporting that intrinsic motivation, even after your engagement is long over.

This section also addresses an issue that often occurs in workshops or engagements: Participants are excited and involved with the content *during* the event, but once they leave the room and return to the reality of their day-to-day lives, they do not put what they learned into practice. Whether it is because there are just too many competing factors vying for their attention, not enough knowledge or support to actually use what they learned, or no system in place to follow up, in essence their time with you is lost if it never gets used.

Before you read this section, take a minute to reflect on the following questions:

What methods do I employ *during* my engagements to encourage participants to use the information or knowledge I am presenting?

_____

_____

_____

---

[38] See (Pink)
[39] (Bénabou and Tirole)

What *systems* do I teach or put in place to help participants use what they are learning/gaining from my engagements after they leave?

_____

_____

_____

_____

_____

_____

Do participants actually use what we cover? How do I know?

_____

_____

_____

_____

_____

_____

CHAPTER 45
Create an Action Plan

The concept of using habit formation to improve one's life has been steadily gaining momentum, with an ever-increasing number of books and research articles pointing to the effectiveness of the approach in helping people with everything from eating healthier to running a better business. [40] In the work I do with my company, Spark Decks, I use the principles of habit formation to support staff, parents, and students to "learn by doing." Like most people in the habit-formation camp, we understand that trying to make too big of a change all at once can be so overwhelming that it never happens. The remedy, therefore, is to focus on micro-practices, meaning, small steps or actions that get repeated and reflected on over time until they simply become, well, a habit.

If you, like me, are interested in capitalizing on the research around how habit formation works and how you can integrate it into your engagements and participant action plans, here are a few helpful tips and things to know that will support you along the way:

❑ **Emphasize choice**. As with all things Transformative, letting participants generate and choose which habits they want to form is essential because the motivation to follow through increases when the choice is put into their own hands. We generally present the habit-formation options in one of two ways, either by:

a. inviting participants to generate a list of micro-practices and then asking them to choose one or two to focus on that they are most excited about, or

b. by presenting a set of micro-practices (in the form of our Spark Decks), and giving them time to consider which of the ideas presented they are most excited about, and how they would modify the ideas to suit their needs, before selecting one or two to try out.

The opposite of this, by the way, would be a supervisor telling all staff that they MUST do some new practice or program, which, unfortunately, is what very often happens.

❑ **Inspire**. The "initiation phase" of habit formation really matters. This means that the way that you launch the process needs to be done thoughtfully and in such a way that it inspires people to embark on the journey. Participants must be sufficiently motivated by the end of the workshop or meeting to actually follow through with forming a new habit. Everything within this book is about getting to that point. The idea is that through using Transformational Facilitation strategies (like creating a welcoming environment, using active learning strategies, and empowering participants), participants feel ready and confident to take on a new challenge.

❑ **Keep it simple.** Keeping the habits both positive and manageable is key. This means that the options must be behaviors or strategies that participants are working *toward*, not something

---

[40] (Lally and Gardner)

they are trying to "quit," and also that they must be bite-sized and truly doable.

Some examples of doable habits might include things like,

→ "Use a silent attention-getting signal to get students' attention,"
→ "Start every meeting with a brief check-in question," or
→ "Pause for ten seconds after you pose a question before calling on someone to answer so that everyone has a few moments to think."

Some examples of less actionable suggestions might include things like,

→ "Don't yell at students,"
→ "Create a system for gathering feedback from meetings," or
→ "Don't let one participant derail your meetings."

❑ **Generate a plan.** Once participants have selected what habit they are going to form, help them by asking them to write it down along with when and how they are actually going to do it. Research shows that habits are most successfully formed when they are associated with a cue. So, for example, "I will use my attention-getting signal *any time my students start getting too noisy.*" Creating a full written plan around potential stumbling blocks and, similarly, potential resources that can support the habit development, is also useful. In this example I would encourage the participant to reflect on how they would teach students about the signal, what they plan to do if/when students don't respond to the signal, etc.

❑ **Offer Support.** Accountability buddies and opportunities for self-monitoring are another way to offer support. The buddy can either be yourself or a peer who the participant can check in with on a regular basis to share how the process is going and become a source of encouragement and sounding board to work through challenges.

It is important to note here that research suggests that habits are best formed through intrinsic motivation,[41] not external rewards, meaning activities like being praised for effort are more effective than handing out chocolate to a staff member who is using an attention-getting signal. Positive feedback and self-monitoring through a buddy system or similar check-in process can help bolster a participant's satisfaction with the habit-formation process and lead to continued efforts to make it stick.

While I love traditional action plans (who, what, when), using micro-practices works really well with an experiential learning cycle, as I write about in the following chapter. Combining the concept of a bite-sized action with a cycle of reflection is usually the action plan I encourage participants to embark on when they leave my workshops. As in, choose a micro-practice, try it out, reflect on how it went, adjust, and repeat.

In fact, this is the cycle I am encouraging you to use with this book! If you haven't already started, now is the time to try out the action planning template in the Appendix on page 159.

---

[41] (Ryan and Deci)

CHAPTER 46
Reflect

In Chapter 43, I wrote about incorporating reflection time and questions into your meetings or workshops so that participants can pause to think about how what they are learning or hearing relates to their own experience or prior knowledge.

In this chapter I'd like to focus on how reflection can be used as a learning tool *after* participants have left the engagement, and particularly as it relates to Experiential Learning theory.

If you are not familiar with Experiential Learning, in short, it is the idea that one way to learn deeply and meaningfully is by doing. In fact, it is often referred to as *"learning by reflecting on doing."* The theory was first published by David Kolb in the early 1980s and is very useful for those of us thinking about how to support people who don't always have the time or access to sit in a traditional class to learn what we need to know. [42]

There are four stages in the Experiential Learning Cycle, and a learner can start in on the cycle at any stage:

1. **Concrete Experience**: This is often referred to as the "Do" stage. For participants I am facilitating, this experience can come from two places, a) their experience in their job or b) an experience I lead them through during the engagement.

2. **Reflective Observation**: This is where the learner intentionally "reflects on" what they have experienced.

3. **Abstract Conceptualization**: Also referred to as "Think," this is the point at which a learner draws conclusions or outlines a theory based on what they have experienced and reflected on.

4. **Active Experimentation**: In this "planning" stage, the learner decides what to do and then tries their theory out as the process now starts all over again.

Here is an example of how I do this in an actual workshop.

1. **Concrete Experience**: I set up a hands-on activity, let's say it's a math game played with a partner, that participants all engage in.

2. **Reflective Observation**: After they have played the game, I ask them to reflect on the experience. Questions I might ask are, "What did you like about playing the game? What math skills did you learn? What interpersonal skills did you have to use?"

3. **Abstract Conceptualization**: At this point I will ask participants to evaluate what makes the game a good way for their students to learn math concepts (or not!). I might ask,

"Would this game be challenging for your students? Why or why not?" "In what ways could you change the game to make it easier or harder for students with differing levels of math skills?" "How does this game reinforce math learning?"

4. **Active Experimentation**: Here is where participants are asked to decide on how they will bring what they just experienced and reflected on back to their students. Usually I invite participants to actually make a commitment in writing, on some kind of action plan template where they state, "What I will try" and, "When I will try it," and that includes any materials they may need to gather to get ready.

One of my favorite opportunities is when I am brought in to do a "series" with a group of staff. The wonderful thing about a series is that it gives time, between sessions, for participants to engage in stage 1 after having been led through stages 2-4 during the initial workshop. In our second meeting, I can start right in on stage 2 by asking participants to share what they tried and repeat the process anew!

As I have mentioned before, at Spark Decks we provide a Notebook with a template for participants to use that helps them continue this Experiential Learning process when we, as facilitators, are not around. This is something you may also want to try. On a simple handout you can ask questions like:

> → What did you try?
> → What worked?
> → What did you learn?
> → What would you do differently if you did this activity again?
> → What will you do next?

In this way, you are guiding participants through the cycle and encouraging them to bring the learning process into their everyday practice for years to come. If you haven't already done so, an action step for you from this chapter is to use the reflection sheet in the Appendix on page 160 after the next strategy you try out from this book, so that you have an opportunity to see for yourself how meaningful reflection can be.

CHAPTER 47
Offer Continued Support

I seem to be on dozens of mailing lists these days. Most of the time, I just delete the emails without even opening them. It's a rare catchy subject line that will actually cause me to pause to take the time to click. Similarly, my inbox is full of "unread" messages, which are actually messages I've read and then decided to mark unread so I remember to follow up on them later. Much later.

So it comes as a bit of a surprise to me that when I send out follow up emails after workshops, they have a fairly high open rate. Especially because I am certainly not creating catchy subject lines. I like to think that this open rate has something to do with the authentic connection that people made with me and their co-participants, and that they actually want to access the tools and resources I had promised to send them.

Because that is what I include in my follow up emails. In each workshop or event, I make sure to collect everyone's contact information and let them know that I will be sending them the Facilitator's Agenda (for those who want to bring it back and run the workshop for their staff), clean copies of the handouts (because you know they are interactive and therefore the ones they used in the workshop are already used up), and links to relevant information or tools I mentioned during the engagement. I also include all of my contact information, with an invitation to reach out if they have questions or need anything else.

(Sidenote: I use Mailchimp to add their emails to a mailing list that includes a category for which workshop they attended. I like sending emails using a service like this because a) I think it has a better chance of getting past their spam filters, b) I can see how many people actually open the email and even which links within the email got the most clicks, and c) it enables me to add attendees to my general mailing list where I send out information on upcoming workshops I think they may be interested in.)

I love it when a participant actually replies to my follow-up email with questions or comments. To me, running a two-hour workshop or conference session often feels like I am simply planting a seed, with no chance of ever seeing what kind of plant will grow from it. Having a way to continue connecting with the people who I spent learning time with allows me an opportunity to continue watering those seeds, and sometimes even getting to see the plant, as participants often return for additional workshops that they learn about through my mailing list or send follow up email questions.

As of this writing, there are over 1,200 people on my mailing list, and almost every one of them is someone I have personally met through running a workshop, conference session, or at an event. That's a lot of people to have a personal connection with! I hope that these people in some way also feel a connection to each other, since we are all doing similar work and travel in similar professional circles, crossing paths sometimes years later, running into each other and laughing with surprise that we are still here, working to create positive change in the world.

Being a Transformational Facilitator doesn't end when people leave the room you all were in together. Being a Transformational Facilitator means you are always there for people. It is a big commitment, but if you've gotten this far, I'm pretty sure it is a commitment you are ready to make or have already made.

I encourage you to start keeping a mailing list or think about ways you can continue connecting with people after they leave your workshop or meeting. Think about the following questions as you plan your connection:

What kind of follow up documents or support can I offer that will enable people to carry on the work and learning that we started in our time together?

What is actually useful that won't end up being deleted before it is read?

How can I continue to bring a feeling of help and encouragement to those who actively choose to work with me and attend my session?

CHAPTER 48
Create Networks

One of the greatest parts of Transformational Facilitation are the relationships that get formed between participants during an engagement. "Participants will learn *and share*..." is the start of each of my objectives on every agenda I write. Each of my agenda items is designed to foster participant interaction, connection, and learning from each other, with the aim of having everyone in the room talk to everyone else in the room at some point, whether that be one-on-one, or in a small group, even when we are a large group.

To make this happen, it's very important to designate time for people to introduce themselves to each other before each activity (name, where you work, what you do). It is easy to rush through an icebreaker or team-building activity and forget to have people introduce themselves; believe it or not, as I stated before, people will not automatically do it if not prompted! My first suggestion for this chapter, therefore, is to make sure you leave time and remind people to introduce themselves to their partner or small group before starting in on working together or discussing the prompt.

When people are allowed time to introduce themselves in pairs or small groups in this way, they immediately start to make connections. In fact, I often find I have to cut their conversations off, as they start to digress about who they know at each organization, or topics related to the fact that they may have similar job titles and/or responsibilities. If people are really seeming to want to foster these types of connections, you have several options:

❏ **Encourage people to exchange contact information.** The most straightforward way to do

this is by letting people know during the "introducing time" that they are welcome to trade business cards. However, there are other fun ways to make this happen. For example, you can give people a sheet of paper that has room to write the name of who they met, their email and phone, and the reason why they are excited to stay to in touch. People keep these papers and at the end of the event, while you are creating action plans, you can suggest that people make a commitment to follow through with contacting at least one person from their paper.

❏ **Start an email chain.** As I mentioned in the previous chapter, I like to send out a follow-up email via a service. However, if you are confident that your note will get past spam filters and that people won't misuse everyone's emails, sending out your follow up email with everyone on it, and even including a contact list that people can opt into during the workshop, will allow people to connect with each other even if they didn't gather contact information during the event.

❏ **Create a virtual group**. An even more direct option is to set up an online group, for example, a closed group on Facebook, where people can connect to ask each other follow up questions, post their successes, or share information about their work. Not everyone is engaged in social media (especially for work), but it is an option if you think your participants will use it.

I encourage you to think about how you are fostering inter-connectedness between participants, even ones who may already work together or know each other. Staying connected and getting to know each other encourages deeper connection to the work and the topic you are covering, since we are social by nature and often motivated when we feel we are all working towards a common purpose.

Before you move on, reflect for a minute: What ways can I find to help everyone stay connected?

_____

_____

_____

NOTES

CHAPTER 49
Create Closure

End with a word.

This is something I do to wrap up pretty much every workshop, so I thought I'd spend a minute talking about the what, how, and why of the ever-useful quick closing circle.

What: A short activity to provide closure to a workshop or meeting. I have heard this called many different names, from the "Last Word," to a "One Word Whip Around." The basic idea is that all participants stand in a circle and share ONE WORD (or a very short phrase) that describes how they are feeling about the day's topic.

How: To run the activity, after everyone is assembled in a circle, ask everyone to take a deep breath (or stretch) and spend a minute thinking about one word that describes how they are feeling about the topic at hand. After thirty seconds, share that it is fine to repeat a word if someone else says what you were planning to say, and it is also fine to pass if you do not want to share.

Now ask for a volunteer to start by sharing their word, this person then gets to point left or right and the word-sharing continues quickly around the circle in that direction until everyone has had a chance to share.

Why: There are many reasons why I like to end sessions with this activity!

❑ **It provides closure**. Too often I see meetings ending without any real sense of having ended fully, mostly because time has run out and people need to get on to the next thing on their calendar. Just like saying, "goodbye" when you leave for work or drop your kids off at school, people like to be able to have a moment of connection, however brief, before switching gears. This activity allows for that.

❑ **It is quick**. As with saying "goodbye," the one word and rapid-sharing nature of this activity means that you don't need to save a lot of time for it. Even if you only have one minute left, you can do this activity!

❑ **It helps get a read of the group**. If everyone is sharing words like, "confused, frustrated, unsure," then you know you will need to follow up, because clearly something is off. If the words that are being shared are more along the lines of, "motivated, excited, inspired," you know you are on the right track and can plan for the next engagement accordingly.

❑ **It helps leave things on a positive note**. If people are sharing negative words (as per the example above), you can end with a few words thanking everyone for sharing and assuring them that you will be following up to make sure that their questions and feelings of frustration get addressed in a follow-up session.

❑ **It leaves the room with participants' voices hanging in the air**. Yet again, this is an opportunity for everyone to hear themselves and their thoughts broadcasted to the group, a central element of Transformational Facilitation.

If you don't already have a closing practice, I encourage you to try this one. It can also be modified, for example, by first asking participants to write their word on a sticky note which they post on the wall before sharing their word, or by sharing with a partner first, if time allows. Spend a minute thinking about how you currently close your engagements. How might you use this activity, or a similar activity, to introduce the practice of providing closure?

NOTES

CHAPTER 50
Use "Ink, Pair, Share"

Towards the end of a workshop, class, or meeting, facilitators often solicit information from participants about what they learned, questions they still have, etc. I applaud everyone for introducing the questions and welcoming the feedback. The WAY this is done, however, can have a stronger impact on participants when enacted through a Tranformational Facilitation lens.

For example, I can't count the times I've been to a meeting, workshop, or class where, toward the end, the teacher or facilitator asks the group a question (or if they have any questions) and then calls on on the first few hands to respond. I discuss the problems with this in Chapter 26, but I know for myself what often happens is that instead of listening to the people who were called on, my mind wanders to my own half-finished idea that wasn't quite ready enough for me to raise my hand and share. What we also now know happens from a facilitator perspective is that you run the risk of a single voice responding for long periods of time, and/or asking questions that may not be relevant to the larger group, or that are off-topic.

The method I am about to share addresses all of these problems at once. It's generally called, "Ink, Pair, Share," which has a nice ring to it and makes it easy to remember, but I often also refer to it as pair-share or turn-and-talk, which are both similar activities.

❑ **First, pose your prompt.** For example, "What question is foremost in your mind right now?" or "What is one important idea you heard during this class that you can incorporate easily into your work?" Make the question prompt very clear and answerable. If you are using a PowerPoint, put the question in there for your visual learners.

❑ **Next, invite participants to spend a few minutes responding to the prompt in writing.** This is the "ink." One fun thing to do is provide an index card. This is less intimidating than a whole sheet of paper since it can only accommodate a few sentences. Having the thoughts on an index card also means that you can collect the cards, or have participants exchange them, as I will explain in a moment.

❑ **Pair**. Once you've given ample time for participants to finish their thoughts in writing (remind them that they have one minute left, then thirty seconds left, then to "finish up your final thought"), ask them to turn to a partner, or find a partner who they worked with at some other point in the workshop, and share their response to the prompt with that partner. Remind everyone that each person should have _ minutes to share, and remind them to switch once that time has elapsed.

❑ **After the "pair," it is time for the "share."** There are so many engaging ways this can be done! Here are just a few to get you started:

→ Ask participants to share out one interesting idea they heard from their partner, so they are not sharing what they just SAID, they are sharing what they just HEARD. This is critical as it serves as an editing mechanism. Partners will filter out any responses that were not relevant or meaningful! Repeating what they just heard also keeps the response more brief than if the response was shared by the original participant. See how this makes your work as a facilitator easier? Of course, it also encourages active listening, something that is always in need of reinforcement. In fact, you may want to prompt participants prior to the pairing, letting them know that they will be sharing what they hear, so that they know to listen attentively.

→ Invite participants to trade index cards after they have shared and then find a new partner. With their new partner, they now share what their first partner shared. Again, this is similar to the idea above, but now EVERYONE is sharing what their partner said.

→ Up the game and make it even more fun by asking everyone to switch cards with their new partner, as above, and repeat the process yet again. Now ideas are flying around the room, everyone is talking, and true "pollination" is taking place. One thing you may hear people say as this is happening is, "Oh, yeah, it's like another idea I just heard..." So now they are making connections between ideas and all kinds of learning is happening.

→ Ask participants to tape their index cards (or, you may want them to write on sticky notes for this one during the "ink" portion of the activity) to the wall. Invite people to stand up and find a response that is similar to what they responded and pull it off the wall. Now invite them to turn to a partner and share the card they pulled. You can also then ask for a few volunteers to share the one that they pulled and why.

I am sure you can think of even more ideas for what to do with those cards! The point is that using "Ink, Pair, Share" in this way helps bring all voices into the room, rather than just a few active participants. Carve out time for this in your agenda - you will need at least fifteen minutes. It may seem like a long time to spend in reflection, but the payoff in terms of total participation is certainly worth it.

CHAPTER 51
Collect an Exit Ticket

The difference between an evaluation and an "Exit Ticket" is that evaluations capture participant opinions and takeaways (including quantitative questions), whereas Exit Tickets are strictly qualitative and more similar to an assessment.

Here are my thoughts and tips on using Exit Tickets:

❑ **Decide whether the tickets will remain anonymous**. It is up to you whether you want to have people put their names on their tickets or not. Do you want to know what each individual learned or are you more interested in looking at themes? People are often more open in their responses when their name is not attached, but if you want to know where each individual is at, then putting their names on the tickets is the only way to go.

❑ **Make it big.** The easiest way to do a ticket is to **post the question** up on a chart paper or a slide and then ask everyone to write their response on an index card. I usually find five minutes to be enough writing time. If you want to get fancy, I've found some cute templates, like this one, that I've used. People get a kick out of writing on a giant ticket, and having fun helps get those creative juices going. [43]

❑ **Make sure everyone turns in their ticket** in before they leave. At a number of events I've attended, I've seen organizers or facilitators give participants something in exchange for their ticket, like a book, swag, or other incentive. This puts the "ticket" into Ticket. Simply stand by the door and collect the ticket as people leave,

---

[43] (Abramis)

(either handing them something in return, or not).

❑ **Ask clear, open-ended questions.** I discuss reflection question types in Chapter 43, but here is a list of questions you might specifically want to include on an Exit Ticket:

> → Do you think [solution to topic] will work in your workplace? Why or why not?
> → What next steps do you plan to take based on what you learned/discussed today?
> → What questions do you still have about [topic]?
> → How would you explain [topic] to a co-worker?
> → What made today's session different from other meetings/workshops you've attended?

❑ **Decide how you will review the data.** There is no sense in asking for Exit Tickets if you don't intend to use them! One way to make sense of them is by sorting them into piles by similar responses. This strategy can help patterns emerge that may be useful to you in planning future sessions, whether for the same group or a new group. As I mention in the following chapter, I also really like using the ATLAS data protocol [44] for Exit Tickets.

If you aren't already doing any kind of formal evaluation or reflection at the end of your sessions, today is the day to start! Exit tickets are a good first step if you are looking to begin incorporating evaluation into your work because they include just one question, take only a few minutes, and are fairly straightforward to review. Give it a try and then reflect on how it informs your work.

---

[44] Based in part on the work of the Leadership for Urban Mathematics Project and the Assessment Communities of Teachers Project. The tool also draws on the work of Steve Seidel and Evangeline Harris-Stefanakis of Project Zero at Harvard University. Revised November 2000 by Gene Thompson-Grove. Revised August 2004 for Looking at Data by Dianne Leahy.

CHAPTER 52
Use Evaluations

It feels like everything we do now is followed by a survey. Like your experience using our app? Rate us! How was your doctor's visit? What did you think of this restaurant? Let us know your thoughts!

It's hard to tell if this is just an industry gone wild, or whether people actually are planning and pivoting based on the data they are collecting. It's probably a mix of both. Certainly, we know that people choose products and services based on ratings they read.[45]

There are actually many reasons to solicit feedback from participants. Here are my thoughts and suggestions on when, how, and why to start asking your participants to provide feedback at the end of each meeting, workshop, or event.

❏ **Use the data.** First, and foremost, I strongly recommend that you only ask for feedback if you intend to actually use it. Asking for feedback simply to make people feel like they're "having a say," is a nice idea, but it is not authentic.

❏ **Ask quantitative questions and calculate percentages.** I like to include the meeting objectives with a likert scale, so that participants can rate each one. I usually frame the statement as, "I learned what [topic] is and feel ready to implement it." or "I had an opportunity to share and learn what steps I can take to [topic]." The choices for participants on the scale usually run from "Strongly Agree" to "Disagree." I can then take the responses and turn it into a percentage.

So, for example, if eight out of ten participants said they "Strongly Agree" with the statement, I can say, "80% of respondents felt that they..." This helps with the next suggestion:

❏ **Look for patterns.** After each engagement, I read through the evaluations and look to see if any themes emerge. Is there an objective that many participants rated as not having learned? Is there a persistent call for less or more of something? While individual perspectives are also helpful, getting a big-picture feeling for where you can improve usually hands me my first next step and leads any future adjustments. This can be done with quantitative questions as outlined above, but can also be done with qualitative questions, as outlined below.

❏ **Ask open-ended questions, too.** While a rating is useful to get a snapshot, digging a little deeper with a couple of open-ended questions can be really eye-opening. Some questions I like to ask are:

> → What is one thing you plan to bring back from this session?
> → What is something you really liked/appreciated about the session?
> → What is a suggestion you have for improving the session?

---

[45] (Vega) and (Otar)

❏ **Choose the format.** I greatly prefer paper surveys for groups that are less than thirty. The reason is because with online surveys, which are usually sent out after the event is over, I don't get as high of a return rate. Handing out a paper survey and collecting it at the end of your session will usually result in much more feedback. I emphasize that the feedback is anonymous and encourage everyone to be honest in their responses.

For online surveys, which I recommend if your engagement has over thirty people, I usually use a Google Form, although Survey Monkey gives you more options if you want a more sophisticated survey. The Google Form lets me do a likert rating that can be turned into a nice pie graph right in the application. This makes pattern-forming easier with a large number of surveys, which can be difficult to tally by hand.

❏ **Give people enough time to complete the evaluations.** I recommend at least five minutes of silent time for participants to do the evaluation. When I run out of time and the evaluations are rushed, of course I don't get nearly as in-depth or thoughtful responses. Schedule this into your agenda so that you really set aside the time.

❏ **Share the data with participants.** Remember those Google pie graphs? I love to share those back with participants or their supervisors. It enables us all to see what people feel they learned, and where more learning still needs to happen. I love using the ATLAS Looking at Data protocol from the School Reform Initiative (see Appendix, page 162), to do this. to do this.

❏ **Prepare yourself.** The first step in the ATLAS protocol mentioned above is predicting what you think the data will contain. Take a minute before looking at participant evaluations to do a self-evaluation, (What went well? Where could you have done better? What do you think participants enjoyed? What do you think they would want to change?). Now see if your predictions align with how participants actually responded.

❏ **Keep an open mind.** I know that sounds obvious, but it is easy to feel defensive and create retorts in your head when reading feedback (I know you *think* you want more time to write, but three-quarters of the group was already finished, so sometimes you just have to move on!). If you are feeling rushed or stressed, wait until you have a calm minute and are in a better headspace to review the data—it doesn't have to happen right way.

❏ **Use the data to advertise your services or make a case for why you are offering what you are offering.** I include participant feedback/quotes on my website, newsletter, social media, and when inviting people to workshops. Since my evaluations are always anonymous, I simply attribute the quote to "workshop participant."

If you are not already soliciting feedback at the end of your sessions, try it out. If you are already doing it, reflect on the suggestions above and think about how you can improve what you are already doing to make it an even more authentic and meaningful part of your work. I have included a sample feedback survey in the Appendix, on page 161.

Postscript: Facilitate Everywhere

You did it! You made it to the end of the book. I am so curious to hear what you have tried, learned, gained, failed at, and tried again. Are your spaces more inclusive? Do people feel empowered? Are you changing the world one engagement at a time? I have been pondering these same questions while you've been using this book, and I am sure we'd have fun conversations and notes to compare. I hope we have the opportunity to do so and encourage you to get in touch. I am a real person, after all!

This book began as a Spark Deck, which came out of all of the work that Oscar and I had done and seen done over our many years of working with school districts, organizations, and city agencies. We were following in the footsteps of all of the great facilitators who came before us, alongside us, and up behind us. The ideas in this book are not really "mine," and I do not claim ownership of them: I have simply collected them here for you, along with some examples of how it can be done, and some simple framing to make the process easier. I hope you have found it both useful and inspiring.

I spend a lot of time thinking about how to expand what I have learned and experienced in the meetings and workshops I facilitate into everyday life, so I want to close our time together with a chapter on how Transformational Facilitation can also work in your everyday life. Here are my thoughts on how to bring some of these concepts to your family or celebratory get-togethers. Because all events benefit when we think about maximizing participation, connection, and joy.

❑ **Know your audience.** As we have learned, when you are wanting to successfully facilitate a meeting or workshop, knowing your audience is crucial. The same is true about showing up to or hosting a holiday gathering or party. For example, last Mother's Day our family was invited to a party at a friends' house. I knew there would be a lot of kids there. I also knew that my kids get very excited (read: rambunctious) when they are around groups of other kids. So I went out and bought a bunch of craft supplies for everyone to make a couple of no-mess projects. It kept the masses busy, sitting still, and working all together. If I hadn't known there would be lots of other kids there, I might not have thought of bringing the supplies, because my kids would be happy to just play with the host's child and his toys. Knowing that there would be a crowd of little ones that would benefit from being creatively occupied was key. Any information you can gather about who will be there will help you plan accordingly.

❑ **Commit to taking the first step.** I don't know about you all, but even I, generally known as an outgoing and chatty person, can feel very shy and reluctant to start up conversations with people I don't know. In fact, my history of party-going often would find me simply sitting on a couch waiting for someone to sit down next to me and thereby force introductions. Not so anymore. I know that when I enter a meeting or workshop, helping people break the ice with other participants can make all of the difference in whether someone has a positive experience, or can learn anything. So, before I head out to my holiday soirées, I make a personal note to reach out to people I see standing by themselves, looking uncomfortably at the floor, or, yep, sitting quietly on the couch like I used to do - even, and especially when I am not the host (because we all know the host has enough to do to get those delicious hors d'oeuvres out onto the table!).

❑ **Plan ahead**. I never walk into a meeting or workshop without a detailed Facilitator's Agenda. And, while I don't pretend to plan out what I am going to do at a holiday party I am attending, I do aim to put a basic framework on it. For example, if I know it's going to run late, I bring my kids' pajamas with me, so they can change before we leave and fall asleep in the car ride home. If the party has a long window, I think about whether showing up towards the beginning or the end would help our day run more smoothly. Any article you read on dieting over the holidays will tell you to eat before you arrive, or even to plan out a meal once you show up, so that you're not mindlessly snacking on those rich cheese plates all afternoon. While it may be time-consuming and a stretch for your brain to think ahead in this way, in the end you will feel less exhausted (and over-full) from the event.

❑ **Be a host(ess) with the most(ess).** Anything you'd think of doing when you are facilitating a workshop works equally well when you are the host of your own gathering. Nametags, Do-Nows (e.g. here's where to put your coat, here's a drink, check out what I'm serving for dinner, etc.), and facilitated introductions (as in, "I've been wanting you to meet my friend Alice for quite some time!"), all go a long way to making the experience awesome for everyone.

❑ **Now flip it around.** The funny thing is, your instincts for party-going and hosting may be stronger than your instincts for Transformational Facilitation. So, as you are attending all of your get-togethers during the year, my suggestion for you is to think about what it is about these gatherings that makes you feel good, loved, and cared for. Think about what it is you do to help them run smoothly, without major meltdowns or not enough dip. Make a note of those things, and then bring them into your workshops and meetings. Because everything that makes a party great, makes a meeting or workshop even better!

With love and gratitude,
Eva

Professional Learning Community Guide

I am excited that some of you reading this may have chosen to use this book in your professional learning community! Here are a few suggestions for how to get the most out of this book with your group.

☐ **Determine how many times you will meet and for how long.** If you are meeting over the course of a school year, a monthly meeting would work great because in each month you can cover one of the sections. I outline a scope and sequence based on a school year below.

☐ **Plan out what you will cover in each session.** Use my example scope and sequence to help you plan your time together, but note that I only list a few key points. It is up to you to work with your group to develop each agenda!

☐ **Model the strategies.** This is the perfect opportunity to try out everything you are learning about! Some things you may want to try include:

→ Selecting a different PLC member to facilitate at each session
→ Planning out who will bring snacks and who will be the DJ for each session
→ Creating a full Facilitator's Agenda for each session
→ Developing a set of community agreements (Chapter 22) that you bring to each session
→ Using at least one or two strategies from the book in each session, and being transparent about the strategy you are using
→ Asking for and allowing time for feedback at the end of each session. Use that information to plan the next session
→ Creating accountability buddies for people to stay on track with trying out the strategies between sessions

☐ **Celebrate**. Learning needs to be fun and Transformational Facilitation is meant to be a joyful experience. Use your PLC sessions as opportunities to celebrate each other's milestones (e.g. birthdays), and successes, (Did you see one of your colleagues do a great facilitation job last week? Give them a shout out!).

NOTES

Professional Learning Community Scope and Sequence Example

→ **September**: Topic - What is Transformational Facilitation and What Does it Mean To Me?
- ❑ Icebreaker
- ❑ Introduce the PLC and complete the pre-survey, which can be found in the Appendix on page 164.
- ❑ Read the Introduction and FOF Chapter and pair-share any or all of the following questions (or come up with your own questions!):

> → What does Transformational Facilitation mean to you?
> → How do envision this helping your work?
> → What are you most fearful of as you think about becoming a Transformational Facilitator?

- ❑ Closing Activity
- ❑ Homework: Read Section One before the next meeting.

→ **October**: Topic - Why Does Being Prepared Matter and How Can I Better Prepare?
- ❑ Icebreaker on an opening reflection question. You can pull questions from Chapter 36 or 43, make up your own, or use these:

> → What idea popped out at you the most from this section and why?
> → What idea is something you are already doing?
> → What idea is one that was new to you that you'd like to try?

- ❑ Create an Action Plan for something each participant will try out. Use some of the strategies outlined in Chapter 45 and the template found in the Appendix on page 159.
- ❑ Closing Activity
- ❑ Homework: Read Section Two before the next meeting.

→ **November**: Topic - What Does Safety Mean and How Can I Foster That for Participants?
- ❑ Icebreaker on an opening reflection question similar to last month's meeting.
- ❑ An activity that addresses the reflection questions from the introduction to Section Two:

> → What makes me feel comfortable in a meeting, class, workshop, or event?
> → What makes me feel uncomfortable in a meeting, class, workshop, or event?
> → In what ways do I already help the people around me feel comfortable?

- ❑ Closing Activity
- ❑ Homework: Read Section Three before the next meeting.

→ **December**: Too many holidays, take a break and have a party instead!

→ **January**: Topic - How Can We Empower Participants?
- ❑ Icebreaker on an opening reflection question similar to previous month's meeting.
- ❑ Try out Peer Coaching (Chapter 23)

- ❑ Closing Activity
- ❑ Homework: Read Section Four before the next meeting.

→ **February**: Topic - How Can We Use Active Learning Strategies to Energize and Engage?
- ❑ Icebreaker on an opening reflection question similar to prior meetings.
- ❑ Model a number of the strategies
- ❑ Closing Activity
- ❑ Homework: Read Section Five before the next meeting.

→ **March**: Topic - How Do We Motivate Action?
- ❑ Icebreaker on an opening reflection question similar to prior meetings.
- ❑ Peer coaching (again!)
- ❑ An activity that addresses some or all of the reflection questions from the introduction to Section Five:

> → What methods do I employ *during* my engagements to encourage participants to use the information or knowledge I am presenting?
> → What *systems* do I teach or put in place to help participants use what they are learning/gaining from my engagements after they leave?
> → Do participants actually use what we cover? How do I know?

- ❑ Closing Activity
- ❑ Homework: Create a personal action plan.

→ **April**: Topic - Celebration and Close
- ❑ Icebreaker on an opening reflection question similar to prior meetings.
- ❑ Activity that outlines next steps (Will the group continue? If so, how?)
- ❑ Post-survey (found on page 165 of the Appendix).
- ❑ Closing Activity that emphasizes all accomplishments!

Appendix

Troubleshooting Guide

Here are some places to start when the going is tough. Use the blank lines to add in your own trouble spots and note down the related chapters.

✓	Issue	Chapter
	Engagements veer off topic	2, 4
	Meetings go on too long	4, 35
	Participants arrive late or underprepared	3
	Participants check cell phones often, have side conversations	1, 8, 22, 29
	Room is quiet, no one volunteers to speak when invited	20, 23, 26, 35
	One person dominates the conversation	30, 34, 35
	People do not think creatively, are not solution-oriented	25, 28, 42, 43
	Participants do not use what is shared during the engagement, no follow through	45, 47, 48
	Participants talk over each other, argue across the room	15, 19, 20
	Participants complain about having to attend the engagement	1, 27, Section 4
	Participants complain about information overload	7, 36, 37, 42, 43
	People feel exhausted after the engagement	8, 9, 16
	A/V and/or technology malfunctions	37
	Participants do not feel comfortable sharing their ideas	14, 17, 18, 19, 20

In the Spark Decks Model:

1. We assist participants in identifying their **personal learning goals**.

2. We help participants learn and share new ideas, and encourage them to **modify** the ideas to suit their abilities and circumstances.

3. We challenge participants to try out one or two small micro-practices.

4. We provide toolsfor participants to **reflect** on the effectiveness of their efforts, and repeat the process.

www.spark-decks.com

Action Planning Template

The issue I want to address	What I plan to try	When I plan to try it	What I will need (resources, tools, etc.)	Who I can ask for help

Reflection Page

WHAT WORKED?

WHAT DIDN'T WORK?

WHAT DID I LEARN?

WHAT WOULD I DO DIFFERENTLY NEXT TIME?

Participant Feedback Sample Survey

Title of Worshop, Date
PARTICIPANT FEEDBACK SURVEY

By completing this evaluation, you are helping ensure that future professional developments will continue to improve and be more useful for you. Thank you for your feedback!

What is something new you learned today that you are excited about?	
What do you plan to try when you get back to your site?	
What suggestion do you have for us about this workshop?	

In this session...	Strongly Agree	Agree	Disagree	Strongly Disagree
I understand [objective] and know how to apply it				
I shared and learned strategies related to [objective]				
I am ready to implement [objective] and have concrete next steps.				
I understand how to use [objective] and have ideas for bringing it back to my work.				

ATLAS
Looking at Data

Learning from Data is a tool to guide groups of teachers discovering what students, educators, and the public understand and how they are thinking. The tool, developed by Eric Buchoveckjj is based in part on the work of the Leadership for Urban Mathematics Project and the Assessment Communities of Teachers Project. The tool also draws on the work of Steve Seidel and Evangeline Harris-Stefanakis of Project Zero at Harvard University. Revised November 2000 by Gene Thompson-Grove. Revised August 2004 for Looking at Data by Dianne Leahy.

1. Getting Started
   - The facilitator reminds the group of the norms.
   - The educator providing the data set gives a very brief statement of the data and avoids explaining what she/he concludes about the data if the data belongs to the group rather than the presenter. *Note: Each of the next 4 steps should be about 10 minutes in length. It is sometimes helpful for the facilitator to take notes.*

2. Describing the Data (10 minutes)
   - The facilitator asks: "What do you see?"
   - During this period the group gathers as much information as possible from the data.
   - Group members describe what they see in data, avoiding judgments about quality or interpretations.
   - It is helpful to identify where the observation is being made- e.g., "On page one in the second column, third row..."
   - If judgments or interpretations do arise, the facilitator should ask the person to describe the evidence on which they are based.
   - It may be useful to list the group's observations on chart paper. If interpretations come up, they can be listed in another column for later discussion during Step 3.

3. Interpreting the Data (10 minutes)
   - The facilitator asks: "What does the data suggest?" Followed by, "What are the assumptions we make about students and their learning?"
   - During this period, the group tries to make sense of what the data says and why. The group should try to find as many different interpretations as possible and evaluate them against the kind and quality of evidence.
   - From the evidence gathered in the preceding section, try to infer: what is being worked on and why?
   - Think broadly and creatively. Assume that the data, no matter how confusing, makes sense to some people; your job is to see what they may see.
   - As you listen to each other's interpretations, ask questions that help you better understand each other's perspectives.

4. Implications for Classroom Practice (10 minutes)
   - The facilitator asks: "What are the implications of this work for teaching and assessment?" This question may be modified, depending on the data.

- Based on the group's observations and interpretations, discuss any implications this work rnight have for teaching and assessment in the classroom. In particular, consider the following questions:
  - o What steps could be taken next?
  - o What strategies might be most effective?
  - o What else would you like to see happen? What kinds of assignments or assessments could provide this information?
  - o What does this conversation make you think about in terms of your own practice? About teaching and learning in general?
  - o What are the implications for equity?

5. Reflecting on the ATLAS-looking at Data (10 minutes) Presenter Reflection:
  - What did you learn from listening to your colleagues that was interesting or surprising?
  - What new perspectives did your colleagues provide?
  - How can you make use of your colleagues' perspectives?

Group Reflection:
  - What questions about leaching and assessment did looking at the data raise for you?
  - Did questions of equity arise?
  - How can you pursue these questions further?
  - Are there things you would like to try in your classroom as a result of looking at this data?

6. Debrief the Process (5 minutes)
  - How well did the process work?
  - What about the process helped you to see and learn interesting or surprising things?
  - What could be improved?

Protocols are most powerful and effective when used within an ongoing professional learning community and facilitated by a skilled facilitator. To learn more about professional learning communities and seminars for facilitation, please visit the School Reform Initiative website at www.schoolreforminitiative.org.

Professional Learning Community Pre-Survey

	Strongly Agree	Agree	Disagree	Strongly Disagree
I know what I need to do, and feel comfortable getting prepared for a workshop/class/meeting/event.				
I understand how to help participants feel safe in the spaces I facilitate, and am able to achieve this during my engagements.				
I know how, and actively use strategies to empower participants, and am able to step back in the spaces I facilitate.				
I consistently use active learning strategies and am able to keep all participants fully engaged during my sessions.				
I am able to motivate participants towards action, and people walk away from sessions I facilitate confident in their next steps and able to act on them.				

What is something you do well when you facilitate?	
What is something you struggle with when you facilitate?	
What is something you hope to get out of using this book and/or this Professional Learning Community?	

Professional Learning Community Post-Survey.

	Strongly Agree	Agree	Disagree	Strongly Disagree
I know what I need to do, and feel comfortable getting prepared for a workshop/class/meeting/event.				
I understand how to help participants feel safe in the spaces I facilitate, and am able to achieve this during my engagements.				
I know how, and actively use strategies to empower participants, and am able to step back in the spaces I facilitate.				
I consistently use active learning strategies and am able to keep all participants fully engaged during my sessions.				
I am able to motivate participants towards action, and people walk away from sessions I facilitate confident in their next steps and able to act on them.				

What is something you now are better at as a result of using this book and/or being part of this Professional Learning Community?	
What is something you are still struggling with and want to continue working on in your facilitation?	
Did using this book and/or this Professional Learning Community help you? If so, how?	

NOTES

Gratitudes

I always feel especially grateful to my grandmother, Harriet, who had the most open mind and heart of anyone I have ever met and set the standard for love and acceptance as high as it could go. To my mom, dad, and brother, Ethan, for always helping me believe that anything is possible and forever supporting me so I could reach that anything. Special love and thanks to my husband, Hudi, and kids, Rafi and Felix, for listening, cheering me on, playing all that music, and always giving me hugs.

To Oscar Wolters-Duran, for dreaming up Spark Decks with me and for being my business and thought-partner in this work for the past six (!) years. To all of the extended network of Spark Decks family, especially Natalie, Brock, Gabby, John, Becca, and Robert, for allowing me into your organizations and schools to work with your staff and for supporting the dream of participant-centered professional learning through practicing it yourself. I am continuously humbled and deeply in awe of the transformative work you are doing for young people, and truly learn something new and inspiring from you every day.

To everyone I've worked with who has modeled the way, especially my beloved colleagues at SFUSD, Dre, Ali, Ann, Jen, Karen, and Yashica; the whole team at DCYF, for continuing to bring me back year after year; Lynn and Stacey who I first met at CNYD;

Zak at CalSAC; the team at ACOE; and the teammates I've worked with at OUSD, HUSD, WCCUSD, and so many other districts. It feels incredible to be in your company and feel like a part of your leadership that continues to raise the room at every opportunity.

To all of the people who helped make this book a reality, especially Julie Lake for going above and beyond in providing critical feedback, Talya Sanders and Katie Crouch for editing so that people can actually read it without getting completely tripped up by misplaced commas, and Adria Husband, for making sure what I am offering is mindful of bias. I am immeasurably lucky to count you brilliant women in my circle of friends. To Diana Shea and Courtney Pinkerton, for paving the way and sharing your book-publishing wisdom. To everyone who has provided feedback and advice on everything from the cover design, to the title, to marketing: Marge, Molly, John, Mualimu, thank you.

To the creative team, for building, beautifying, and launching this baby: Amy, Lila, Angelica, Arturo, and Morgan; it truly takes a village.

And to you, dear readers, for rolling up your sleeves to get the work done, and for wanting to do it better than ever. Together we are going to change the world, one engagement at a time.

Bibliography

Abramis, David J. "Play in Work: Childish Hedonism or Adult Enthusiasm?" *American Behavioral Scientist*, vol. 33, no. 3, 1990, pp. 353–73.

American Association of University Women. *Short-changing Girls. Shortchanging America: A Call to Action*. American Association of University Women, 1991.

Amit, Elinor, et al. "An Asymmetrical Relationship between Verbal and Visual Thinking: Converging Evidence from Behavior and FMRI." *NeuroImage*, vol. 152, 2017, pp. 619–27.

Ashton, Maxie, and Lanie Varga. *101 Games for Groups*. Psychological Corp, 1998.

Bénabou, Roland, and Jean Tirole. "Intrinsic and Extrinsic Motivation." *Review of Economic Studies*, vol. 70, no. 3, 2003, pp. 489–520.

Bloom, Benjamin S. *Taxonomy of Educational Objectives, Handbook 1: Cognitive Domain*. Addison-Wesley Longman Ltd, 1956.

Boser, Ulrich. *Learn Better: Mastering the Skills for Success in Life, Business, and School, or How to Become an Expert in Just About Anything*. Rodale Books, 2017.

—-. "Talking to Yourself (Out Loud) Can Help You Learn." *Harvard Business Review*, 2017, https://hbr.org/2017/05/talking-to-yourself-out-loud-can-help-you-learn.

Chen, Ying, et al. "Parental Warmth and Flourishing in Mid-Life." *Social Science & Medicine*, vol. 220, 2019, pp. 65–72.

D'Agostino, Fred, et al. "Contemporary Approaches to the Social Contract." *The Stanford Encyclopedia of Philosophy*, edited by Edward N. Zalta, Metaphysics Research Lab, Stanford University, 2019, https://plato.stanford.edu/archives/spr2019/entries/contractarianism-contemporary/.

Deming, Vasudha K. *Big Book of Leadership Games: Quick, Fun Activities to Improve Communication, Increase Productivity, and Bring Out the Best in Employees*. McGraw-Hill, 2004.

Doran, G. T. "There's a SMART Way to Write Management's Goals and Objectives." *Management Review*, vol. 70, no. 11, 1981, pp. 35–36.

Duhigg, Charles. "What Google Learned From Its Quest to Build the Perfect Team." *The New York Times*, 2016, https://www.nytimes.com/2016/02/28/magazine/what-google-learned-from-its-quest-to-build-the-perfect-team.html.

Dweck, C. S. *Mindset: The New Psychology of Success*. Random House.

Fernandes, Myra A., et al. "The Surprisingly Powerful Influence of Drawing on Memory." *Current Directions in Psychological Science*, vol. 27, no. 5, 2018, pp. 302–08.

Gardner, Howard. *Frames of Mind: The Theory of Multiple Intelligences*. Basic Books, 1983.

Gray, Dave, et al. *Gamestorming: A Playbook for Innovators, Rulebreakers, and Changemakers*. O'Reilly Media, 2010.

Jones, Alanna. *Team-Building Activities for Every Group*. Rec Room Publishing, 2000.

Karlesky, Michael, and Katherine Isbister. "Understanding Fidget Widgets: Exploring the Design Space of Embodied Self-Regulation." *Proceedings of the 9th Nordic Conference on Human-Computer Interaction*, ACM, 2016.

Knowles, Malcolm. *Andragogy in Action: Applying Modern Principles of Adult Learning*. Jossey-Bass, 1984.

—-. *The Adult Learner: A Neglected Species, Third Edition*. Third Edition, Gulf, 1984.

Knowles, Malcolm S. *Self-Directed Learning: A Guide for Learners and Teachers*. Association Press, 1975.

Koh, Aloysius Wei Lun, et al. "The Learning Benefits of Teaching: A Retrieval Practice Hypothesis." *Applied Cognitive Psychology*, vol. 32, no. 3, 2018, pp. 401–10.

Kolb, David A. *Experiential Learning: Experience as the Source of Learning and Development*. Prentice Hall, 1983.

Kondō, Marie. *The Life-Changing Magic of Tidying Up: The Japanese Art of Decluttering and Organizing*. Ten Speed Press, 2014.

Kristiansen, Per, and Robert Resmussen. *Building a Better Business Using the Lego Serious Play Method*. John Wiley & Sons, 2014.

Lally, Phillippa, and Benjamin Gardner. "Promoting Habit Formation." *Health Psychology Review*, vol. 7, no. 1, 2013, pp. 137–58.

McCrindle, Andrea R., and Carol A. Christensen. "The Impact of Learning Journals on Metacognitive and Cognitive Processes and Learning Performance." *Learning and Instruction*, vol. 5, no. 2, 1995, pp. 167–85.

Miller, Brian. *Quick Brainstorming Activities for Busy Managers: 50 Exercises to Spark Your Team's Creativity and Get Results Fast*. First Edition edition, AMACOM, 2012.

Milligan, Colin, et al. "Workplace Learning in Informal Networks." *Journal of Interactive Media in Education*, vol. 1, no. 6, 2014.

Ogle, Donna M. "K-W-L: A Teaching Model That Develops Active Reading of Expository Text." *The Reading Teacher*, vol. 39, no. 6, 1986, pp. 564–70.

Otar, Chad. "Council Post: How Review Sites Can Affect Your Business (And What You Can Do About It)." *Forbes*, 2018, https://www.forbes.com/sites/forbesfinancecouncil/2018/10/05/how-review-sites-can-affect-your-business-and-what-you-can-do-about-it/#205c49bb266a.

Pink, Daniel H. *Drive: The Surprising Truth About What Motivates Us*. Riverhead Books, 2011.

Pinkerton, Courtney. *The Flourish Formula: An Overachiever's Guide to Slowing Down and Accomplishing More*. Bird in Hand Press, 2017.

Reaven, Marci. *Toward a More Perfect Union In an Age of Diversity: A Guide for Building Stronger Communities through Public Dialogue*. City Lore, Inc., 1997.

Ryan, Richard M., and Edward L. Deci. *Self-Determination Theory: Basic Psychological Needs in Motivation, Development, and Wellness*. The Guilford Press.

Scannell, Mary, and Mike Mulvilhill. *Big Book of Brainstorming Games: Quick, Effective Activities That Encourage Out-of-the-Box Thinking, Improve Collaboration, and Spark Great Ideas!* 1 edition, McGraw-Hill Education, 2012.

Schulkin, Jay, and Greta B. Raglan. "The Evolution of Music and Human Social Capability." *Frontiers in Neuroscience*, vol. 8, 2014.

Shelly, Anne Crout, et al. "Revisiting the K-W-L: What We Knew; What We Wanted to Know; What We Learned." *Reading Horizons*, vol. 37, no. 3, 1997.

Siddarth, Prabha, et al. "Sedentary Behavior Associated with Reduced Medial Temporal Lobe Thickness in Middle-Aged and Older Adults." *PLoS ONE*, vol. 13, no. 4.

Siegal, Daniel J. *Mindsight: The New Science of Personal Transformation*. Bantam, 2010.

Slater, Don. *An Innovative Use of Fidget Toys in a University Classroom*. SoTL Commons Conference. Vol. 45, 2011.

Vega, Nick. "Here's Why User Reviews on Sites like Amazon Are Such a Big Deal." *Business Insider*, 2017, https://www.businessinsider.com/amazon-reviews-greatly-impact-online-shopping-sales-2017-3.

Vogel, Susanne, and Lars Schwabe. "Learning and Memory under Stress: Implications for the Classroom." *Science of Learning*, vol. 1, no. 1, 2016.

About the Author

Eva Jo Meyers is the co-founder of Spark Decks, a company that focuses on "micro-practices" and embedded workplace learning, and also leads her own consulting practice, through which she provides professional learning support to school districts, city agencies, and nonprofits. Prior to these positions, Eva coordinated expanded learning programs for SFUSD, served as an education director with the Boys and Girls Clubs of SF, worked as a bilingual Spanish 2nd/3rd grade teacher, and carried out research for a year as a Fulbright Scholar in Thailand, studying the influence of culture on pedagogy. She recently took a break from life in the U.S. to spend a year teaching pre-service teachers at Yangtze Normal University in Chongqing, China. She holds a BA in Visual Arts with a concentration in Social Activism, a Masters in Humanities and Leadership, and a K-12 teaching credential in art. She is the song-writer for the band, Making Dinner, and has released four albums. In all things, she believes that equity and inclusion are imperative for creating a thriving world and future. Stay in touch at www.raisetheroom.com.

About the Artist

Tla'tollis
From '*Leyendas Otomíes*'
by Arturo Moh Méndez

Arturo Moh Méndez created the cover artwork for Raise the Room based on an indigenous legend from the Otomí People in la Sierra Norte de Puebla, Mexico:

"*There's a series of populations in the mountains of La Sierra Norte that lived very far away from one another, as a result, people barely developed the ability to speak because they wouldn't have others to speak to. That is why many of them started speaking to the deer, rabbits, and birds around them. They realized how particularly beautiful it was when birds gathered atop the trees to sing. Little by little, they realized they could use the birds' language to communicate at long distances amongst humans, and more and more people started doing so. And that is how birds taught humans to talk and to listen to each other.*"

There are populations who still use this language, which Arturo learned when he was a child playing with his uncles and cousins, without knowing that it was a language. In the image of the story, the glyphs coming out of the birds' mouths are called **Tla'tolli**, a symbol that can be found in indigenous writing of Mexico from before the Spanish arrived. In many ways, this is the first speech bubble that existed. You can listen to examples of people conversing here: http://bit.ly/whistle_language.

To learn more about 'Leyendas Otomíes' and the legends that Arturo has been collecting, illustrating, and animating, visit arturomendezsf.com